Funding for this item provided by

FRIENDS OF
WILLIAMSBURG REGIONAL LIBRARY
Support the library - www.wrl.org/friends

Critical Acclaim for Michael Frayn

'Michael Frayn is the most philosophical comic writer – and the most comic philosophical writer – of our time.'
– Michael Arditti, *Daily Mail*

'Bernard Shaw couldn't do it, Henry James couldn't do it, but the ingenious English author Michael Frayn does do it: write novels and plays with equal success.'
– John Updike, *The New Yorker*

'Frayn, author of some thirteen novels and sixteen plays, is a literary double threat.'
– *The Boston Globe*

'A master of intellectual mystery masquerading as ripping popular entertainment.'
– *The New York Times Book Review*

'[A] writer who likes to pull the rug out from under your feet while offering you the most seductive of smiles.'
– *The Seattle Times*

'[M]y own favorite British humorist.'
– Kurt Vonnegut, Jr.

'There are two Michael Frayns . . . One is the master of the comic caper, the antic trickster and entertainer who sets off laughs the way an automatic rifle shoots bullets – very many, very quickly. The other is a less frenetic, more measured, more thoughtful soul, who impresses with his depth and wise understanding of everyday human foolishness.'
– *Newsday*

MICHAEL FRAYN

THIRTY SHORT ENTERTAINMENTS

MATCHBOX THEATRE

VALANCOURT BOOKS

First published in Great Britain by Faber & Faber, October 2014
First published in the U.S.A. by Valancourt Books, February 2015
Copyright © 2014, 2015 by Michael Frayn

Published by Valancourt Books, Richmond, Virginia
http://www.valancourtbooks.com

Library of Congress Cataloging-in-Publication Data

Frayn, Michael.
[Plays. Selections]
Matchbox theatre : thirty short entertainments / Michael Frayn.
pages ; cm
ISBN 978-1-941147-50-4 (*acid-free paper*)
I. Title.
PR6056.R3A6 2015
822'.914–DC23
2014029384

ISBN 978-1-941147-50-4 (*trade paperback*)
Also available as an electronic book

Cover design and interior illustrations by M. S. Corley

Set in Janson Text

10 9 8 7 6 5 4 3 2 1

MATCHBOX THEATRE

• • • PRESENTS • • •

THIRTY SHORT ENTERTAINMENTS

Welcome to Matchbox Theatre!

Would you please take a moment to check that all mobile phones and other electronic devices are switched on? Your calls are important to us!

Photography is permitted throughout. Please feel free to obstruct the aisles. Leave luggage unattended! Talk among yourselves! Eat! Drink! Sleep! Snore! Storm out in the middle, if you feel like it, letting your seats thump up and crashing the panic bolts as you go!

MATCHBOX THEATRE IS A SUPPORTER OF NATIONAL ENERGY-SAVING AND TRAFFIC REDUCTION POLICIES.

SLEEPERS

A tomb. Sir Geoffrye de Frodsham and Lady Hilarye lie motionless side by side, a little dog at their feet.

Several years go by. Then the thump of rock music filtered through masonry.

Geoffrye? I know you're awake. You're not breathing. Don't pretend you're asleep. No one could sleep through that noise . . . Geoffrye!

   – Um?

They've started again. You'll have to do something about it. You'll have to go down to the crypt and talk to them.

   – They'll stop in a minute.

They're going to go on all night . . . At least bang on the floor!

– *You* bang on the floor.

You're the one with the sword . . . It's driving me mad!

– They'll get to some prayers in a minute.

Prayers? At a disco?

– It's not a disco.

It's the disco!

– It's choral Evensong.

What are you babbling about?

– It's choral Evensong! He does a special early one for young people! In the crypt!

On Saturday night?

– On Sunday afternoon.

It's Saturday night.

– It's Sunday afternoon.

You've lost all sense of time. How can it be Sunday afternoon? It's dark!

– It's winter!

It's summer!

– It's winter!

Since when has he been doing choral Evensong in the crypt?

– Since 1997.

I've never heard any choral Evensong in the crypt.

– You were asleep.

You're telling me I slept through *that?*

– You slept through the Second World War . . . Anyway, it's stopped. I told you.

It'll start again.

– Um.

Don't be silly. You're not asleep. I can tell from the way you're lying.

– How am I lying?

Not like someone who's asleep. Nobody lies like that when they're asleep.

– Like what?

All stiff and unnatural. With your hands pressed together. Not even you.

    – Take a pill.

I don't know why you're doing all this thing about sleeping if it's the afternoon.

    – Haven't you got a pill?

I haven't got a pill.

    – Maybe the dog ate it.

Don't start on the dog.

    – That dog shouldn't be on the tomb.

She keeps my feet warm.

    – No wonder we can't sleep. We've all got fleas.

I've got to have *something* warm next to me.

    – What's that supposed to mean?

Nothing.

    – Nothing. Oh.

Why, what did you think it meant?

    – Nothing.

That's all right, then.

    – You're always saying things that mean nothing.

Better than never saying anything at all, which is what you're always doing.

  – I'm always never saying anything? 'Always never' – that's an interesting formulation. So that's what I'm doing now, is it? Never saying anything?

Not *saying* anything, no. Not *talking*.

  – So, I'm lying here in silence . . .

By the sound of it.

  – What – *then*? I was waiting for you to reply.

So now what are you waiting for?

  – Doomsday.

It's funny. Everyone thinks we're the perfect couple.

  – Who thinks we're the perfect couple?

All the people who come to look round the church.

  – That's because you never open your mouth when anyone's here.

Nor do you.

  – Obviously not. When anyone's here.

Such as me.

– I talk to you a lot more than that dog ever does.

Yes, well, if you're not going to say anything sensible let's go to sleep.

– I thought you couldn't sleep?

I can't! I've been lying here awake since 1934 . . . ! What?

– I didn't say anything.

No, but you're thinking it. You might as well say it. I can't sleep with you lying there thinking.

– What am I thinking?

You know what you're thinking. And it's not true! I did *not* sleep through the Second World War!

– Well . . . perhaps it was the First World War.

Also you keep moving about.

– I am lying absolutely still . . .

You're grinding your teeth.

– How can I grind my teeth while I'm talking?

Listen to you! Grind, grind! Like millstones!

– That's my eyelids. I was closing my eyes.

Any moment you'll get one of your cramps.

   – I never get cramp unless I think about it.

Then we'll see you move!

   – If you're trying to make me think about it you're wasting your time.

You'll be off this tomb like spit off a hotplate.

   – I am *not* thinking about it!

You'll be bouncing round the nave like a pea in a whistle . . . Any moment now . . .

   – Agh!

There! I told you! The whole tomb bounced up and down!

   – You're always doing this to me!

Stumping about. Banging on the floor. They'll hear you in the crypt!

   – I thought you *wanted* me to bang on the floor?

Not when they're quiet! You'll set them off again! Funny, isn't it. *I* ask you to bang on the floor – oh, no. But then as soon as it happens to suit *you* – oh, well, that's different – bang, bang, bang!

– Agh!

Go to the doctor! Get some pills! Other men don't behave like this! Other men can manage to lie still on their tombs for a few centuries without all this performance! The last time was in the middle of a service! We had people here! You made an absolute spectacle of yourself. Everyone thought you'd gone completely mad. They all got out of the church as fast as their legs would carry them. He had to have the whole place exorcised!

– That was ages ago.

It was the Sunday before last!

– It was the second Sunday in Lent. I remember the sermon.

Oh, you remember the sermon? I wonder you could take it in, while you were hopping round clutching at everyone for support.

– Lent 1885.

1885?

– 1885.

You're getting confused. 1885 was when the bat droppings fell on you.

– The bat droppings fell on me, *and* I got cramp.

It must have been a busy year for you.

     – It *was* a busy year for me.

Not as busy as 1923. When your nose went.

     – When my nose went? That wasn't 1923! That was
       1723!

1723?

     – We're losing track, old girl. One century's getting
       remarkably like the next.

Oh, Geoffrye! What's happened to us?

     – What do you mean, what's happened to us? Noth-
       ing's happened to us! That's the trouble!

You never look at me these days.

     – I don't see you looking at me.

No, because you never look to see whether I'm looking
or not.

     – Stiff neck.

You used to look at me.

     – Let's get some sleep.

We used to go out together.

– Out?

Sometimes. Occasionally.

– What, down the road to St Ethelbert's, to see Ethelbert?

We used to look in on Henry and Catherine, in that little side chapel.

– Very boring couple.

Only after Cromwell.

– Not much fun, talking to people with no faces.

Before that, though. We used to dance.

– Dance? When was this?

A long time ago. Before we got so stiff.

– Oh. Then.

You were a good dancer.

– Was I?

When you got going. That first evening, though . . .

– You wouldn't dance with me!

You wouldn't ask me! You simply stood there! Dumb-struck! Like an effigy already! We might have been stuck standing up there instead of lying down here, for the next six hundred years!

– But in the end . . .

We danced.

– And then what happened?

We were standing in church.

– Yes. Over there somewhere.

In front of the altar.

– And there was music.

There were bells.

– The church was full of people.

There was a ring.

– And there was a kiss.

And we walked through the church among the people . . .

– And then . . .

There was a bed.

– We lay down on the bed.

Like this.

  – And something happened.

Yes. Something happened . . .

  – Our joints began to grow stiff.

Yes, but before that . . . Sometimes you used to . . .

  – Used to what?

You didn't always have your hands pressed together.

  – No, well, you sometimes used to move your hands
    a bit.

You used to put one of your hands on me.

  – Like this?

Like that.

  – Nice. Nice?

Nice.

  – Very nice . . . Then what happened?

We had fourteen children. But once . . . once . . . on
Maundy Thursday . . .

  – Oh, Maundy Thursday.

You remember?

   – I remember that Maundy Thursday.

Maundy Thursday 1674.

   – 1674 . . . That was a good year . . . I enjoyed 1674 . . .

I think I've unsqueezed my other hand a bit . . . Geoffrye?

   – Um?

Listen, love . . . Geoffrye . . . ? You haven't gone back to
sleep . . . ? Oh, and now those devils in the crypt have
started up again! Geoffrye! Stop them! Bang on the floor!

   – What? What?

Wake up!

   – I am awake. I was only dreaming I was asleep . . .

COLD CALLING

Congratulations! You have won the . . . And he's hung up on me!

    – Again? That's the third time!

He doesn't even wait till I've got to the end of the sentence! I don't get any further than '*Congratulations! You have won the* . . .' – and wham! Already the phone's back on the hook. What's happened to the world? People used to be so excited when you rang to tell them! They thought it was a real honour!

    – Honour? These people don't know what the word means. Money, money, money – that's all they think about these days.

Yes, then there's the money. You'd think they'd be pleased about the money.

– What – the odd few million kronor? They look in the paper, and there are bankers taking home ten times as much for wrecking the economy! Which one was that? Peace? So he's a politician? Naturally, then. Coining it already. Pay-offs, backhanders. Then off to work for a bank himself. Forget Peace.

But what if he doesn't ever realise he's won?

– Then we're several million kronor to the good. Try one of the others. What's the next one on the computer? Medicine. Try Medicine.

Medicine? Big Pharma? On a royalty from some billion-dollar drug that's killing everyone in Africa?

– Maybe. Or maybe not. Maybe a humble doctor. A saint. Runs an obesity clinic in the jungle. Doesn't want a single krona for himself. But now, thanks to us, he can install flush toilets and flat-screen TVs. He'll be all over you!

Yes, you can joke about it. You haven't got to do it.

– Come on! I'm dialling it for you.

It's not nice, you know, being hung up on all the time. You feel rejected. You feel everyone hates you.

– Don't take it so personally.

I can't help taking it personally! It's something about my voice, isn't it. As soon as they hear it . . . wham!

– Right, you're through. He sounds charming, this one. Modest, hopeful. I don't think this one's going to hang up on you. Off you go.

They all sound hopeful when they pick up the phone. Then . . .

– Get going. He's waiting.

He's going to be the same as all the others . . . *Congratulations! You have* . . . And the phone's back on the hook already. Quickest yet. Look, I don't think I can go on with this job. The stress is really getting to me.

– OK, let's think. Maybe it *is* something about your voice. A bit *too* positive, perhaps, a little *too* encouraging. They think you're trying to sell them something.

How else can you say 'congratulations'?

– So maybe *don't* say 'congratulations'.

Don't say 'congratulations'? What are you talking about? It's in the script they give you!

– Forget the script. Get straight to the money. Where are we? Literature. Perfect. He's, what, a poet or something?

She. Some woman in Lithuania.

– Wonderful. She really needs the money. Economic

collapse. Husband left her. Kids to support . . . OK, I'm dialling . . . Suddenly there's going to be this voice on the phone: 'Our records show that you may be entitled to a substantial payment . . .' Something along those lines . . . I'm through . . . Oh my God! She sounds desperate! Away you go!

Hello! Our records show . . . And wham. I can feel chest pains.

– OK, let's come at it a bit more obliquely. Work up their anticipation . . . What's the next one on the computer? Physics . . . I'm getting it for you . . . Just give your chest a rub – you'll be fine . . . It's ringing . . . He's a scientist, so start with something scientific. Catch his interest. The computer. Start with the computer. Something about his name coming up on the computer. He'll be intrigued.

The computer . . . ? *Hi there! Your name has come up on our computer and* . . . I told you.

– Never mind. His loss, not ours. We're about twenty million kronor up. Three more to go. Where have we got to? Biology?

I think I'm going to take early retirement . . .

– Now, with Biology we'll try something completely different. Something a bit more streetwise. You remember the old advertising maxim? 'Don't sell the steak, sell the sizzle'? So you're not going to tell this Biology guy anything about a prize. You're going to tell him about the trip to collect it! Yes? OK, I'm dialling ... He's in Bangalore. It's hot and dusty. The air conditioning in the laboratory's broken down. He's dreaming of cold and snow. A call from Scandinavia, and already his tongue's hanging out. So then you tell him about the free champagne. The five-star hotels. The world-class gourmet cuisine. The beautiful blonde hostesses ... Here you go ...

This is the very last one I'm going to try ... *Hi there! You have won an exciting free trip to Stockholm* ... And already he's ... No! He hasn't! He's still there!

– What did your wise old Uncle Sven tell you? Quick – 'free champagne, free champagne ...'!

Enjoy beautiful free champagne ... world-class blondes ... five-star hostesses ... Now he's hung up ... No, he hasn't! I don't believe this ... ! *Hello? You're still ...? Oh, thank you! Thank you, thank you, thank you! Thank you for holding! Thank you for listening! You don't know how much this means to me! So, yes, world-class free hostesses ... What? Where do I want to go? Where do I want to go ...? Nowhere! Not me – you! You're coming here! Yes? To Stockholm! The fantastic fairy-tale city often known as the Athens of the North!* Wait, wait. *I'll read you the official citation* ... Where's my piece of paper ...? What a sweetheart! He's hanging on every word ...! *Right. You're really still there ...? Wonderful. I'll take it from the top. The whole script. Is that all right? You've got a moment? You won't suddenly ...? No, OK, here we go, then ... Congratulations! You have won the Nobel Prize for Biology ...! Oh ... Oh, I see. I'm so sorry ...*

– Even this one?

Wrong number. Minicab firm in Malmö ...

CONTRAPHONIUM

... 537 ... 538 ... 539 ... 973 minus 539 equals ... what ... ? Can't do it ... 430-something. So, another 430-something bars before I come in ...

Only I missed a few bars there while I was working that out. You can't count and do mathematics at the same time! How many did I miss? Say half a dozen. And another half-dozen while I worked *that* out ... So we're somewhere around, say, 550 ... 551 ...

Which is still only quarter of the way through Act Two!

553 ... 555 ... People say, 'Oh, lucky you! Going to the opera every night and getting paid for it!' I don't know how lucky they'd feel if they went to the opera and found they'd got a seat at the back of the orchestra pit. Underneath the stage. Playing the E-flat contraphonium. An instrument that no one wants to hear, not even the composer, except for three bars of straight G natural

halfway through Act Two. Followed by another 1,271 bars of sweet FA natural.

Nothing to see from here except the backs of the bassoons. And Fred on flugelhorn at the next desk. I'm getting so fed up with the sight of Fred. Look at him! Forty bars after his last contribution to proceedings, and he's still fiddling about with his tap . . .

567 . . . 568 . . . They say, 'Well, at least you can enjoy the music.' Enjoy the music? When you're trying to count out 973 bars rest inside your head? 573 . . . 574 . . . When you're struggling not to let your mind wander, only you've nothing to think about except 577 . . . 578 . . . Nothing to look at except that little black line on the stave with 973 written above it. And the backs of the bassoons. And Fred. And Fred's maddening, distracting, fiddling fingers. You can't even *hear* the music!

Now I've lost count again . . . ! No, fine, because there goes Fred, off on his next blast, which is my bar 595. Fred always knows where we are. Set my watch by him. Nothing to distract him. No imagination. Never thinks about anything except counting. He's got a maths A-level, of course.

That's where I went wrong. Failing maths . . . Mr Smother said, 'Never mind, Miss Evermore says you try hard in the recorder group – you can do music . . .'

Now he's fiddling with his tap again. Probably got an A-level in plumbing as well.

600 . . . I think. Isn't it . . . ? Must be. At least.

And they all look down on you! All those goody-goodies up there in the strings. Huddling round the conductor like little kids in nursery school sitting on the floor round the teacher. Smug looks on their faces because they're working so hard. Here's us, they're thinking, lucky if we get a bar off in every hundred. Eight semiquavers to the bar, often as not. Sixteen hemisemi. All of us going down with burnout and RSI. And there's that idle so-and-so at the back playing his E-flat contraphonium. Or rather not playing it. He might as well be sitting at home and drawing jobseeker's.

The way that new girl in the violas looked at me in the canteen! I show her how to use the coffee machine, so she doesn't get two shoefuls of latte. 'Oh, how sweet of you!' she says. 'Not at all. Just trying to make you feel at home. Oh – Walter Wendell, E-flat contraphonium . . .' Woof! Turns on her heel – back to the violas! Well, let her try and play this thing, if she thinks it's such a cushy number. She'll get burnout all right. She'll have panic attacks. She'll be on invalidity benefit.

Oh no – Fred again! But that's not till bar 713! We're not at bar 713! We can't be! Can we . . . ? What's everyone else doing . . . ? Nothing happening in the trombones. All quiet in the oboes . . .

Where have we got to upstairs, then . . . ? He's strangling her . . . My God, that's something like bar 1300 . . . !

Hold on . . . *Is* this the one where he strangles her . . . ?

Where's the title page . . . ?

Oh, no, it's that other one. Some kind of funny business in a forest. Moonlight. Falling in love, and whatnot . . . All very beautiful. But do those bastards up there ever think of us down here? They don't, do they! They don't give a damn about us. We have feelings, too, you know! We try to be nice to someone. She turns her back on us. We get bitter. We go out and kill someone.

Fred, probably. Ram his flugelhorn down his throat. I hate the flugelhorn. I hate Fred.

People say, 'But if you don't like sitting there, why don't you go out and have a drink? Just come back a few bars before they get to you, like George and Jack do for their bits on the triangle and the wind machine?' Because that's not the way I was brought up, that's why! If my dad could sit watching the security cameras at a canned pea factory for twenty years, I can surely sit here and watch Fred fiddle with his waterworks for an hour or two.

Fred again – 911 . . . 912 . . . They pay airline pilots a fortune for doing this kind of job. Sitting there bored, bored, bored while all the work's done for you by the computer. Until suddenly everything's flames and smoke and you're falling out of the sky and you don't know where you are and all you know is that suddenly it's all down to *you*.

People say, 'But what's the problem? You can see the conductor, can't you?' Yes, I can see the conductor. He's only about a hundred yards away! 'And he looks at you, doesn't he,' they say, 'when you finally get there? He tips you the wink!' Oh, sure. Half a bar before you come in! Have you ever tried to pick up an E-flat contraphonium at half a bar's notice? This thing weighs as much as your average lawnmower! Try snatching this thing up too quickly and you'll rupture yourself! Plus you've got to get your breath, you've got to get your lips pursed. So by the time he looks at you . . .

Oh my God! He's looking at me . . . ! Quick, contraphonium . . . ! Oh, my back, my back – it's gone again . . . ! Now, breath! Lips . . . ! Help – what note am I playing . . . ? Oh, right . . .

Made it! Just!

Was that beautiful, though, or was that beautiful?

And only another 1,271 bars to count before the next blow.

PROMPTS

Cafe. Two tables. At one table: MR AND MRS HAZEY. *At the other table:* MR AND MRS SHARPE

MRS HAZEY (*to Mr Hazey*): . . . Anyway, I ran into her yesterday in Tesco's and I said, 'Oh, I haven't seen you around recently,' and she said, 'No, we've been away, and you won't believe where we went,' so I said, 'What, not to Spain?' Which is where they usually go, and she said, 'No – Marrakash!' I said, 'Marrakash? What, that place in the desert?' Oh, and she went on and on about it. Marrakash this, Marrakash that. 'You must go to Marrakash! You'll love Marrakash!'

MRS SHARPE (*to Mr Sharpe*): . . . Oh, and on my way to the reading group I ran into Hilary, and she said they'd been walking in Montenegro, which is totally unspoilt, and they came across a derelict sheepfold with the most sublime views which they completely fell in love with, and bought on the spot for an absolute pittance . . .

She stops, her attention caught by something she has heard.

MRS S (*to Mr S, but half-intending to be overheard*): Marrakesh.

MRS H: You'd think no one
in the world had ever heard
of Marrakash.

Marrakesh.

What?

MR S *frowns, embarrassed.*

MR H: What?

MRS H: I thought you said
something?

MR H: No?

MRS S: Anyway, this place
they've found is very close
to the border with Herzego-
vina, so you can fly to either
Ptsk or Sibenik . . .

MRS H: Marrakash!
I said to her, 'I'm not
sure I like the sound of
Marrakash.'

MRS S *freezes again.*

You might prefer the sound
of Marrakesh.

MR S: Sh! They'll hear!

MR H: So we won't be going
to Marrakash?

MRS S: No! You won't be
going to Marrakash! There is
no such place as Marrakash!

MR S (*hurriedly*): And where are Justin and Lucinda thinking of going this year?

MRS S: I don't know, but I don't think it's Marra*kesh*. And it certainly won't be Marra*kash*. I think they're thinking of somewhere more like . . .

MRS H: Lanzarottle. What's wrong with Lanzarottle? Or Terrenife?

MRS S *manages to say nothing.*

MR H: I wouldn't mind going to that other one.

MRS H: What other one?

MR H: That other one that's M something.

Madeira.

Not Madeira. *You* know. Where Arthur and what's her name went.

Mauritius. Martinique.

MRS H: What – Arthur and Annie? You don't mean Magadascar?

MR S *silently entreats* MRS S *to remain silent.*

MR H: Magadascar. I mean Magadascar.

MRS S (*loudly*): No, you don't! You mean . . .

[33]

MR S *claps his hand over* MRS
S's *mouth.*

MRS H *glances round.*

MR S *hastily releases her.*

MRS H *turns back to* MR H.

MRS H: It wasn't Magadascar.
That's where Laurie and
Lou went!

MR H: No, they didn't. It
was Arthur and ... you
know ...

(*at random*) Edie.

MRS H: It was Laurie and
Lou!

MR H: It was Arthur and ... !

Edie!

MRS H: Arthur and Edie?
Who are Arthur and Edie?
You don't mean Arthur and
Edie. You mean Eddie and
... what's she called ... ?
Eddie and ...

(*at random*) Ida.

Eddie and Ida.

MR H: Who are Eddie and
Ida?

MRS H: *I* don't know! You
mean *Freddie.* Freddie and
...

Freda.

Freddie and Freda.

MR H: Freddie and *Freda*? Half these people you keep talking about I've never heard of!

Freddie and Flora.

MRS H: Freddie and *Phyllis*.

(*agrees*) Freddie and Phyllis.

Only Freddie and Phyllis didn't go to Magadascar. They went to Holonunu.

MRS S *utters a strangled cry.*

MRS H (*to* MRS S): Are you all right, dear?

MRS S *coughs and nods.*

MR S: Choked on something.

MRS H (*to* MR H): Only they didn't like it.

MR H: Didn't like what?

MRS H: Holonunu. They didn't like all those geesha-geesha girls.

MR H: What geesha-geesha girls?

MRS H: I don't mean geesha-geesha girls.

MRS S: You mean hula-hula girls.

I'm mixing it up with Haititi.

MR H: Haititi?

MRS H: Where they rub noses with you. Where that painter cut off his ear.

MRS S *utters a quiet, suppressed scream.*

[35]

(*quietly*) Don't look round. I
think they're having a bit of
an arghy barghy.

MRS S: Argy bargy!

MR S: Right. That's enough.

He begins to hustle her out.

Anyway, you won't get *me* to
Holonunu. I'd sooner go to
Marrakesh.

MRS S (*departing, screams*):
Marrakash! Marrakash! Marrakash!

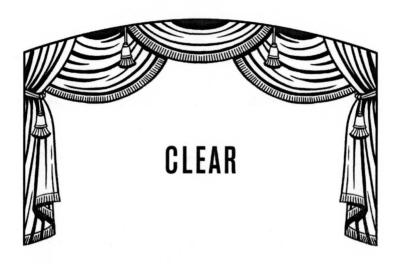

CLEAR

Let me be absolutely clear about one thing.

This is of course what politicians of all persuasions preface their remarks with these days. And when they're not asking you to let them be clear about what they're going to say next they're telling you that they *are* clear, whether you like it or not. Or claiming that they always *have* been.

But what they mean by being absolutely clear is not always absolutely clear in itself. So let me make it clear what *I* mean by it.

I should perhaps make it clear before we go any further that when I say that there's one thing I want to be clear about this is an understatement. There is more than one thing. There are masses of things! The only trouble is that, since I am being so completely clear about them, and since one totally transparent thing looks much like another totally transparent thing, it's difficult to tell one from another.

So one absolutely clear thing at a time. And the one I want to be absolutely clear about first is what I *don't* mean by being clear.

I don't mean being clear like the clear glass door that you don't see, so you walk into it and bang yourself most painfully on the nose;

or clear like a clear road late at night, so you're tempted to put your foot down and drive so fast that you don't notice police cars or speed cameras, and you have to persuade your wife to take the penalty points for you, and everything thereafter gets less and less clear;

or clear like the clear you're in when you've somehow shifted the blame for what you did on to someone else;

or clear like your conscience after you've done this so successfully that you've completely forgotten about it;

or clear like your wardrobe after a good clear-out, when you've thrown away everything that you can't believe you once thought was fashionable, and probably also some things you still want to wear that somehow got mixed up with everything else;

or clear like clear decks, after all your principles and other deck cargo have been washed away or thrown overboard;

or clear like the clear sky that the thunderbolt falls out of.

No, what I mean when I say that I'm absolutely clear about something is that I'm as clear as an empty glass bottle. Not, of course, an empty brown or green bottle, which might still have last night's left-over dregs in it, or a few dead spiders. An empty vodka bottle, say. So that you can see it actually is empty. If you can still see anything after drinking a whole bottle of vodka. Or maybe this is another bottle which is still full of vodka . . . Unless someone's drunk the vodka and filled it up with water . . .

Or with something you bought to spray on the roses to kill greenfly.

But most likely it's full of absolutely nothing at all, like all the other empty vodka bottles in the recycling bin. Which is why it's so absolutely clear. Because nothing can be clearer than nothing!

In fact I am even clearer about this than an empty bottle. I'm as clear as the carefully polished glass plate of the Autocue from which I'm reading these words, and which is so clear that from where you're sitting you can't see it, so you think I'm actually thinking what I'm saying. And which from where I'm standing makes it clear to me just how unclear you are. Totally invisible, in fact. Which is why I'm up here and you're down there.

Let me be absolutely clear about that, if nothing else.

HOW AM I FEELING, DOCTOR?

I'm feeling terrible, doctor!

I don't mean ill – I'm *not* feeling ill – I'm feeling fine. That's why I'm feeling terrible! I'm feeling terrible about troubling you when I'm *not* feeling ill.

I *was* feeling ill. I was feeling terrible. I had this kind of . . . *feeling*. Not *this* feeling, the feeling terrible about troubling you . . . I mean, a physical feeling. Something *here* . . . No, hold on – it was more round the side . . . Or was it the other side . . . ?

I don't mean a pain. It wasn't a pain. It was a kind of . . . *feeling*. A funny feeling. I can't describe it. I don't mean a feeling like a burning feeling, or a tingling, or an itching, or a griping . . . Or feeling sick, or tense, or feverish, or achey, or fluey . . .

I can't remember now quite what it was like. But I

remember that it wasn't like *that*. It was just this . . .
funny feeling.

Which is why I felt a bit *worried* about it. Well . . . not
worried exactly. I didn't feel it was the kind of feeling I
had to *worry* about.

I was just worried in case I *ought* to be worried. I was
just worried about coming to see you and then finding
that it *wasn't* anything worrying – or not coming to see
you and then finding it *was* something worrying that
I hadn't come to see you about because I was worried
about coming to see you and then finding that it *wasn't*
anything worrying.

I know how you must feel about me taking up your time
telling you about this funny feeling when I can't tell you
what the funny feeling was. Not knowing what *I* feel
doesn't mean that I don't know what *you* feel!

And I know how you must feel about me taking up yet
more of your time telling you how terrible I feel about
taking up your time. Particularly when I go on as I am
now and tell you how terrible I feel about taking up even
more of your time still by telling you how terrible I feel
about taking up your time telling you how terrible I feel
. . . about taking up your time . . . about telling you how
terrible I feel . . .

I'll *tell* you how you're feeling, in case you don't know.
A little dizzy. Yes? Confused. Inadequate. Slightly nau-
seous . . .

A little worried that you're in the wrong profession. That you don't understand other people's feelings. That you don't even know what you're feeling yourself until somebody tells you.

At the end of your tether. In need of a doctor . . .

Prematurely aged. Looking forward to the end of the day. To retirement. To death . . .

I know, doctor, I know – you're feeling terrible. And of course you're feeling terrible about feeling terrible when what's making you feel terrible is someone who's feeling terrible themselves. Someone who's feeling terrible about feeling terrible. Someone who's feeling terrible about making *you* feel terrible . . .

Take these pills three times a day, doctor. And if you're not feeling any better in a few days' time I'll come and see you again. By which time, with any luck, you'll have completely forgotten what the trouble was.

FINISHING TOUCHES

Darling, you know how much I appreciate the way you're always . . . well . . .

> – . . . helping you, yes, but don't be silly, darling – I love helping you.

. . . always helping me, particularly when I'm saying something, and I . . . you know . . .

> – . . . hesitate.

. . . hesitate for a . . .

> – . . . moment . . .

. . . a moment, yes, and at once . . .

> – It's usually only for a fraction of a second, darling.

Exactly. And at once you very kindly try to . . .

    – . . . finish the sentence for you.

. . . finish the sentence for me. Because you're so much . . .

    – I'm not cleverer than you, darling!

. . . not just cleverer, but because you think so much . . .

    – I do think faster, it's true.

. . . faster. And you know how . . . well . . . how . . .

    – . . . to finish sentences.

. . . how . . .

    – . . . how to speak Italian? How to make apple strudel?

. . . how grateful I am. And you're very good at it because you . . .

    – . . . always know what you're going to say.

. . . usually know what I'm going to say. And because, well, it simply . . .

    – . . . saves so much time.

. . . so much time. Or it would . . .

– . . . if you didn't insist on going on and saying it all over again.

. . . if I didn't . . . Exactly!

– Which is a pity, darling, because we could spend the time we saved doing something else, and since you've brought the subject up, I can't help noticing that sometimes when you go on and finish the sentence I've already finished you do it in a way that sounds just a tiny bit impatient.

No, no, it's just that I feel I would very occasionally like to . . . well . . . like to . . .

– . . . get to the end of a sentence yourself . . .

. . . the end of a sentence myself. Just to see what it was . . . you know . . . what it was . . . well, what it was . . .

– . . . like.

Yes, and then also there are times when you . . .

– . . . get it wrong. Of course.

. . . get it wrong, and you make me . . .

– . . . say things that you *weren't* going to say, that's true, and I'm sorry, but then sometimes I'm right, and you *were* going to say them, only you change your mind just because I've said them for you.

[45]

Possibly, though by the time I say what I'm going to say . . .

   – . . . the conversation has usually moved on.

. . . moved on, and you don't notice me saying what I *am* actually saying, and so you go on thinking I've said . . .

   – . . . what I thought you were going to say, I know, but, darling, if what I thought you were going to say was what you *were* going to say, and you only *didn't* say it because I said it for you, then what I *re-member* you saying is what you actually *would* have said if I hadn't said it for you, so it's truer to your intentions for me to remember it that way, and be-lieve me, I don't *enjoy* finishing your sentences for you – I only do it because . . .

. . . because otherwise we'd be here till midnight before I get to the end of even this sentence – and here you might take note, incidentally, that I *can* sometimes finish sentences perfectly quickly . . .

   – . . . if they're someone else's sentences.

. . . if they're someone else's sentences.

   – Though I notice you never finish other people's sentences, only mine.

Only yours, very possibly – but if so that's because I always know . . . *I* always know . . .

– . . . you always *think* you know . . .

. . . what you're going to say . . .

– Only you *don't*, as it happens.

Let's put it to the test then. I know exactly . . . I know precisely . . .

– . . . what I'm going to say next.

' . . . what I'm going to say next.' You've said it. Precisely. Exactly.

– One of these days, you know, darling, I'm going to . . .

. . . strangle me. Yes, unless I get in first, and . . .

– . . . strangle *me*? Is that what you're trying to say? You'd strangle *me*?

I shouldn't need to, darling, because if I *tried* to strangle you, you'd interrupt me, as usual, and . . .

– . . . strangle *myself*, perhaps?

. . . strangle *yourself* – or else get it wrong, as you so often do, and strangle some other poor fellow altogether. Either way it will somehow turn out to be . . .

– Your fault. Well, of course, it *would* be.

Of course, and I shall end up getting . . .

   – . . . as angry as usual.

. . . fifteen years. Though at least that's a sentence I might be able to finish in peace.

STREET SCENE

What the hell is going on? What for pity's sake do you lot think you're up to?

You – yes, I'm talking to you! And you! All of you!

You call this a street scene? It's rubbish!

My God, I spend the entire working day in a sweltering rehearsal room, trying to direct the street scene in our big production number to make it look like a street scene in the real world, then I come out here on the street in the real world, and what do I find? Do I find a street scene? No, I don't! I find a dog's breakfast! A big boring disorganised mess that doesn't look like a proper street scene at all!

I can't leave it like this! It's a public disgrace! So as a concerned citizen I'm offering my professional services pro bono. Which is why I'm standing up here on the roof of this parked car and shouting at you!

Right, phones off! Now, where do we start?

You lot at the bus stop! MAN WITH BORING BROWN HAIR, OLD MAN ON CRUTCHES, WOMAN WITH OBSTREPEROUS CHILD and all the REST OF YOU! You're not *doing* anything! You're just standing there in a straight line . . . !

Waiting for a bus? Well, *show* us you're waiting for a bus, then! MAN WITH BORING BROWN HAIR look at your watch. Turn to WOMAN WITH OBSTREPEROUS CHILD and make a humorous gesture of impatience. OBSTREPEROUS CHILD tug at WOMAN'S coat. WOMAN give OBSTREPEROUS CHILD a clip round the ear. VICAR bend down to comfort OBSTREPEROUS CHILD. OBSTREPEROUS CHILD give VICAR a clip round the ear.

No VICAR? Gina . . . ! Where's my assistant Gina . . . ? Oh, you're there . . . So, Gina, no VICAR! Get Wardrobe. Tell them to give MAN IN T-SHIRT WITH OBSCENE LOGO a clerical collar . . .

And, Gina, hold the traffic noise, will you? I can't hear the music . . . Of course there's music! There's always music!

You two by the letter-box – you're masking people! TALL MAN – be shorter! OBESE WOMAN – lose three stone!

And Gina – call Casting. We want a lot more people who we can look at them and see what they are. A POSTMAN, yes? A CHIMNEY-SWEEP, a NURSEMAID. A few STREET-WALKERS. CLOWNS. CIRCUS PERFORMER ON STILTS . . .

LOVABLE LITTLE DOG comes running down the street . . .

That thing? That's LOVABLE LITTLE DOG? It's a pit bull! Spray it with something . . . !

I don't know – whatever you spray pit bulls with to turn them into lovable little dogs . . . So, it raises its lovable little leg against the lamp-post . . . *Move* the lamp-post, then, so we can all see it . . .

CHEEKY LITTLE BOY . . . Where's CHEEKY LITTLE BOY . . . ? What, him? He's a CHILD DRUG RUNNER! Spray him, spray him . . . OK, he steals an apple off FAT MARKET-WOMAN's stall while her back's turned . . . Stall, stall . . . ! That . . . ? Oh, sure, it's a stall, but those things aren't apples – they're cut-price pornographic videos. Spray them, spray them . . .

Where's YOUNG MAN IN BOATER . . . ? Gina, give YOB IN BASEBALL CAP a boater . . . OK, whistle at PRETTY GIRL walking past! Where's PRETTY GIRL . . . ? You? You're PRETTY GIRL . . . ? Jesus.

Never mind. Press on. Do the best we can. PRETTY GIRL pretends not to notice, then – consternation! She's lost the bag of red rosy apples she bought off the pornographic video stall! Where can it be? Oh, good heavens, YOUNG MAN IN BOATER has found it! He's running after her! Eye contact! Bashful smiles! Romance! Love! He does a little dance step. She copies it . . . We'll choreograph this later . . . The whole BUS QUEUE takes it up . . . The whole street . . .

I'll turn you CHARACTERLESS ZOMBIES into CHARACTER-FUL CHARACTERS if it's the last thing I do. I'll get you

BRAIN-DEAD INANIMATES animated, I'll breathe charm and lovability into every last SOCIOPATH on the street, I'll make you TONE-DEAF APRAXICS sing and dance.

And, Gina, while you're about it, get those TV aerials down . . . Bring on some vintage cars and hansom cabs . . . Street scenes happen somewhere between 1750 and 1945!

Right, from the top, everyone . . .

BUZZ ME

Hello. This is a message for Schphth Thrgphshnik. I hope I've got the right number!

I'm calling with regard to the Ghrthphsqurw thing on Thursday the schlrhthieth. I was told by Schrggthwk Thwvghrvtkdk that you'd know all about it, so I assume I don't need to spell it out.

I'd be grateful if you could call me back as soon as possible on – and I'll say this quickly so that you can call me back sooner: Oh-two-oh-eight-one-two-nine-four-seven-eight-three. I'll say that again, and faster still so that you can call back even sooner: Ohtwooheightone twoninesevenfourthreeeight. Or alternatively, in case you wasted too much time on that number because there seemed to be rather a lot of digits you could almost catch: Ohtwooheighseventhreetphnschnfschnf. Please quote reference number Totally/37Q/random/3339xJZ/ collectionofletters&digits.

But only if it's between 8.30 and 4.35 on a weekday! Because if it's between say 4.35 and 10.27, or after 3.30 on a weekend, at any rate before the shtdteenth of this month or after the schnrth of the following month, then it's better to try: Ohtwoohflglflglschrndltrdleschnckschnck.

Or it may be easier to get me on my mobile, because it's got a number that's very easy to remember: Ohseventhreetwoohgrglschtrpschtrp ... No, hold on ... Not glschtrpschtrp – grglgrflschtrp ... or rather schtrpschrtrgrgle ... Or am I missing a digit somewhere ... ?

Oh, just in case you haven't guessed who this is, it's Schnthph Schmfgth. Not to be confused with Schmfgth Schnthph! You might remember me if only because of my rather unusual name. My parents' surname was Schlrhgh, and they were going to register me simply as Schwrtrpg, so I should have been Schwrtrpg Schlrhgh, which is about as ordinary as you can get. But just as my father opened his mouth to tell the registrar this there was a kind of strange electrical disturbance in the atmosphere, so his voice came out like something on an answering machine, and when my parents got home they discovered he'd written 'Schnthph Schmfgth'. Or 'Schlrthph Schnrlth' – they couldn't read his writing!

Just to make it absolutely clear, I was the person you met at that party given by Thrthrsh Phsthphthr – who I originally got to know through the Society for People with Names and Numbers No One Can Ever Catch on the Telephone, Unless It's Something Wrong with Your Answering Machine.

So call me Back. That's what everyone else calls me. It's a lot easier to pronounce than 'Schnthph'.

TEA FOR WHO?

– *Picture me*
Upon your knee
With tea for two . . .
– And two for tea . . .
– *Just me and you . . .*
– And you and me
Alone!

    – *And no invitations*
    For tiresome relations!
    – Not even your brother . . .
    – *Perhaps my old mother,*
    She's deaf and blind,
    You mustn't mind
    Her, dear.

– Right, tea for three
And three for tea

And that's the lot.
Just three all told
And simply not
Another soul!
– *Yes, but* . . .

> . . . *We must have poor Steven!*
> – Poor Steven?
>> – *He's grieving.*
> *He's grounds for believing*
> *Eve's going to leave him!*
> *A cup of tea*
> *Will make him see*
> *We care.*

– That's tea for four,
Although we swore
No more than three
Would pass our door.
– *But just for me*
One teacup more!
I'll pour . . .

> *Though if we have Steven*
> *We must make it even –*
> *Ask Eve after Steve's been,*
> *Though Eve has deceived him.*
> *It's only four,*
> *And then four more –*
> *That's all!*

– So eight for cake
And cake for eight,
And pots more pots
Of jam, and tons
More toast, and lots
More currant buns . . .
– *I'll toast!*

> *But now we've agreed on*
> *Both Steven and Eve, then*
> *We must have the two friends*
> *They've found as their new friends.*
> *I'll go and bake*
> *An extra cake*
> *Or two.*

– So twice times five
Will soon arrive!
That's tea for ten
And ten for tea.
Just picture *them*
Upon my knee!
My God!

> *– And then there's the Skinners –*
> *They've had us to dinners –*
> *The Peskitts, the Poskitts,*
> *The Thingys, the Whatsits!*
> *We really must!*
> *It's only just*
> *This once!*

– So now it's more
Like twenty-four!
– *No – thirty-two!*
– Or forty-one!
– *It's hard to do*
As big a sum
As this.

      – You start with a twosome . . .
      – *You've soon got a fewsome . . .*
      – A more- and still moresome . . .
      – *The numbers grow awesome!*
      – So shut the door
      And let's be sure
      No more!

– *The bell again!*
Another ten
Have come to call!
– Oh, please, feel free!
It's tea for all . . .
– *And all for tea!*
– Sit down!

      – *I'll buy a new teapot.*
      A serves-forty-three pot . . .
      – And I'll have a teabag,
      A tea-just-for-me bag!
      – *Have tea alone,*
      All on your own,
      Dear?

Yes, picture me,
No you, no we.
Upon my knee
A cup of tea.
Just tea for me
And me for tea – Alone!

OUTSIDE STORY

So, provided the scheme to build low-cost weekend housing on the estate is accepted by the local planning authority, it looks as if the cherry orchard itself has been saved from the axe. More on that later. Now back to our main story, and we're joined by our special correspondent Richard Roving live outside the National Theatre. What can you tell us about the present situation, Richard?

– Well, it's a fine night out here, George, with a bit of a breeze off the river. But inside it's pretty tense. The good news is that they're still in there, and they're still talking. Some of the talking, by all accounts, has been pretty tough – Hamlet himself, I gather, has not pulled his punches. It's been a long evening – this is the feeling here – and it's going to go on for quite a bit longer yet.

Any developments in the situation since we last talked to you?

– Yes, George, in the last act there has been some sort of showdown, I don't think that's too strong a word, between Hamlet and the Queen. We don't know exactly what was said – no one out here is prepared to talk about it – but I gather there was a full and frank discussion of their differences. What we're hoping is that it may have cleared the air a little.

Richard, we've been getting reports of a stabbing involving one of the Queen's advisers. Can you help us on this at all? I gather the victim's name is Mr Harris, or Aris.

– There was some kind of incident, I understand, but my information is that it wasn't serious. We're always hearing lurid stories, of course – if it's not people being stabbed they're being poisoned, or drowned in butts of wine. There was a rumour running round earlier that someone had seen a ghost! I think one has to keep a sense of proportion.

Any sign of an improvement in relations between Hamlet and the King?

– George, it's too early to tell. But I was talking to someone who was inside the theatre in the last half-hour or so, and he said there were plans at court for a bit of a family get-together, which must I think be a good sign. I understand it involves some sort of home theatricals.

No fears that the King might be tempted to take a tougher line?

– Oh, I don't think so, George.

There were some pretty wild and unsavoury allegations flying about earlier.

– Yes, but there is a great determination here not to let the peace process be derailed, and most of the people I've spoken to remain pretty hopeful about the outcome.

There's no sense of *déjà vu* about all this?

– Yes, George, some old hands have been saying, 'We've seen this whole story played out many times before, and if we don't learn from past mistakes we could just end up with a real disaster here.'

So the next few hours could be crucial?

– They could, George, but the King has already brought two younger men on to his team who are known to be close to Hamlet, in a very clear gesture of conciliation. It may or may not be significant that the Prince is to make an official visit to England, which should help to take the steam out of the situation a little.

Is the Prince showing any signs of strain?

– He has been showing some signs of the enormous pressure he is under, yes. He's made a number of major speeches in the last hour or two, but quite what effect they've had on opinion here it's too early to tell.

Is that the Prince we can see now, just behind you?

– No, that's one of the local dossers being thrown out of the theatre by security men. If you'd been here earlier you'd have seen quite a lot of coming and going just behind me there. Quite a lot of stiff drinks being drunk. Quite a lot of visits to the toilets. But things have quietened down in the last few minutes.

So you feel the signs are good?

– I'm pretty hopeful, George, provided they can just keep talking. They've been talking now for the best part of two hours, and the longer they go on the more likely it is we're going to see them shake hands and issue a joint communiqué.

But if the talks *do* break down . . . ?

– Then it's anybody's guess. The consequences are incalculable. We could, I think, see a distinct worsening of relations. We might even end up with the King and the Prince not on speaking terms.

No chance that it could even end in violence?

– Well, we hope it won't come to that! It's in everybody's interest to stay calm and behave sensibly. They'll probably keep us all on tenterhooks until the last possible moment, but the smart money here is on wedding bells before too long.

Richard Roving, thank you. Now, the rest of the news.

Fire broke out this evening in Valhalla, home of many of the world's best-known gods. Local fire chiefs say that the blaze is now under control. And in Spain a wealthy playboy has had the novel idea of inviting a statue to dinner! The statue duly turned up, and by all accounts thoroughly enjoyed its evening out. That's it for now! Have a good weekend.

MASTER OF
THE MOBILE

So this is the message that I am trying to get across to everyone here in this audience tonight. Technology is vital to us. Communications are our lifeblood. We must have the knowhow to take full advantage of them. Let us ensure that we never become slaves of our machines. That we remain captains of our computers. Lords of our laptops. Masters of our mobiles . . .

And at once, of course, someone's phone is ringing . . .

Exactly! Thank you, whoever the culprit is, for such a graphic and well-timed demonstration of the dangers I'm warning against! If we don't know how to control them, our gadgets will take over our lives. Our wonderful new devices for communicating with each other will make communication impossible . . .

Just as this rogue mobile now is . . .

Anyway, whoever it actually is, I think the point has now been made . . . We've all had our laugh, we've all learnt our lesson . . . So if you would now be kind enough to turn it off . . . No need to be embarrassed about owning up, it's very easy to do, we've all done it . . . I'm waiting . . .

You must know whether it's your phone or not . . . !

No? All right. Will *everyone* please check his or her phone . . . ? Actually take it out of your pocket or handbag, like so, and . . .

Oh. Mine.

I'm so sorry. How very embarrassing. Well, it makes my point even more tellingly. I've managed not only to bring an important speech to a halt, but to make a fool of an otherwise perfectly competent politician . . . If only I had been trained in the theory and practice of mobile phone use at school . . . !

Anyway, I've now turned it off. Wonderful. Where was I . . . ?

My wife, in case you're wondering . . . If only *she* had been trained . . . ! Because I *told* her I was speaking this evening . . . Told her over the breakfast table, not over the phone! Communications between husband and wife, of course, are notoriously fallible, even face to face, without any electronics being involved at all . . .

Unless this actually is something desperately urgent . . .

Never mind, on we go. So, yes, masters of our mobiles, emperors of our emails . . .

Though if it's *that* urgent . . . Perhaps I'd better just . . . I'm sorry. Would you excuse me for one moment . . . ? This won't take a second . . . Just in case. Very difficult to speak coherently once you start worrying about something else . . .

Darling, yes, me – but I am actually in the middle of a speech. I am standing up here in front of an audience at this very moment! So unless it's anything too desperate perhaps I could call you back when . . .

The washing machine . . . ? You did what . . . ? Oh no! I told you to get a plumber . . . ! Anyway, if you've turned off the mains, I don't see how . . . You haven't turned off the mains . . . ? So now it's . . . ? Oh, my God! Well – just open the garden door! Let it run out into the garden . . . ! The living-room *door? You've opened the* living-room *door . . . ? Why . . . ? Yes, well, never mind why . . . What's floating . . . ? My tax returns . . . ? It took me all weekend to . . .*

Yes, but there's obviously nothing I can do! I'm not there! I'm here, I'm in the middle of a . . . ! I know, I know, but presumably you've rung the plumber now! So just keep your finger over the end of the pipe until . . .

You've got his number! Of course you have! It's on that list headed 'Emergencies . . .' Just fetch the list . . . ! No, don't take your finger off the pipe . . . !

All right, all right, there's no need to shout. I'm just looking it up . . .

I'm so sorry about this . . . I've just got to find the number of the plumber . . . Though actually you probably find all this rather entertaining. Rather more entertaining than the speech. I don't, really. But you can't keep everyone happy.

Right – 07035 223 924 . . . All right . . . ? And I'll call you again just as soon as I've . . .

Also what . . . ? Keeps ringing? Who keeps ringing . . . ? Which newspaper . . . ? Well, if he rings again, just tell him that it's completely false, and if they print it I will sue him personally for every penny he . . . No, well, then just give him my mobile number. Only tell him not to call now . . . !

And of course she's rung off. I'm so sorry. Though this is a good illustration of what a politician's life is like. One long series of emergencies and ambushes! Is it a wonder that we can never manage to get anything *done* . . . ? Only now I suppose this reporter fellow is going to start phoning . . . Well, it won't affect us, because this time, look, I'm remembering to turn the sound off . . . Or did I turn it off before? Perhaps this is turning it back on . . .

This is exactly what I mean about technology, incidentally . . . It would be at any rate a start if we were all absolutely clear about how to turn things on and off . . .

And there it goes. Of course – it wasn't off, it was on. I'm so sorry . . . At least now I've found one thing out . . .

Hello . . . Yes, it is me, but no, it's not a good moment . . . You'll have to call me back later. Let me just make absolutely clear here and now, though, that the allegation is completely false. I have never even heard of this woman, and in any case she is a notorious liar, a past mistress of deceit, and that is all I have to say on the subject. All right . . . ?

So. Where were we . . . ? At least I'm sure the sound is now definitely off. I'll put it back in my pocket. If it wants to vibrate silently to itself in there then let it – it won't disturb us.

Yes, captains of our computers . . .

One moment . . . I'm so sorry. You probably can't hear it, but it's just touching my left nipple. Which is curiously sensitive – I hadn't realised . . . So when it vibrates there's this terrible tickling . . . It's impossible to think about anything else – it's impossible to keep still . . . Unless I'm having a heart attack . . . I'll have to get it out . . . Yes, not a heart attack – just the phone . . . I'll put it in my trouser pocket instead, look . . .

So – masters of our mobiles . . . Oh . . . Oh . . . ! *Not* the right place to put a vibrator . . . ! This is even more embarrassing . . . Just take it out . . . Though actually . . . I know how to turn off the sound, but I don't know how to stop it vibrating . . . Apart from by answering it. I'm very sorry about all this . . .

Now, look here, I am not going to be persecuted in this way! If you attempt to call me again I will make a formal complaint to the . . . My mistress? *Who told you she was my mistress? I told you she was my mistress . . . ?*

I said she was a past *mistress . . . ! Yes, but not of* mine! *Of deceit . . . ! What do you mean, of deceit as well . . . ? Oh – de Site. What, not Gervase de Site . . . ? But he's my oldest friend! Wait, wait – you're breaking up – I'll have to take this thing outside . . .*

You lot . . . Just phone quietly amongst yourselves . . .

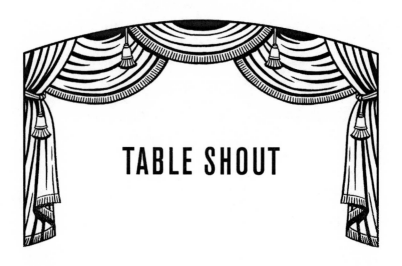

TABLE SHOUT

What do we want?

> – Oh, just a pot of tea, don't you think, darling? And perhaps some toast?

When do we want it?

> – As soon as you can catch the waitress's eye. You must be dying for a cup after your great demo thing!

What do we want?

> – I said: *tea*. Yes? And a few slices of toast. If you're happy with that.

When do we want it?

> – Didn't you hear what I said?

What do we want?

– Darling . . . These demos of yours. You don't think you're perhaps overdoing it a bit?

When do we want it?

– Because I think they may be beginning to affect your short-term memory.

What do we want?

– Tea and toast! Yes? All right? Agreed? Have we got that straight? And if we have, then perhaps also to move the conversation on a little.

When do we want it?

– Before I scream.

What do we want?

– What *I* should rather like, darling, even if you're going to say the same thing twelve times over, is a ban on *shouting* it. Everyone's staring.

Down with the ban!

– 'Down with the . . .'? Oh. Good. Wonderful. A new departure. Well done. I think, on mature consideration, that what I would argue in reply is: Up with the ban!

Down with the up!

– Oh, a real conversation! This is very exciting! So – up with the down!

We won't be gagged!

– Out with the shout!

Out with the out!

– In with the out!

Out with the in!

– Stop the rot! Strain the brain! Fight for longer and more grammatically complicated slogans, containing words of more than one syllable, including qualifications if necessary, and dependent clauses where they help to make the meaning clearer!

Hands off our slogans! Save the monosyllable! No to the dependent clause! Kill the qualifier! Back alliteration! Stand up for reiteration!

– Yes to alliteration! Yes to reiteration! So – where's the waitress? Where's the waitress?

Waitress! Waitress!

– We want waitress!

Why no waitress?

– Waitress now!

And now the waitress!

– Here's the waitress!

Hello, waitress!

– Waitress . . .

Waitress . . .

– Up with the order pad!

Down with the order!

– What did we want? I can't remember!

Tons and tons of toasted buns!

– Bin the buns! Too late for buns! Just lots and lots of
strong brown tea!

Oh, not for me! To hell with tea! Just bring the gin!

– The gin, the gin!

The gin, the gin!

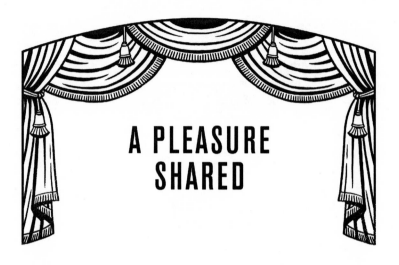

A PLEASURE SHARED

Do you spit? No? You don't mind if I do, though . . . ?
Khhghm . . . Hold on – can you see a spittoon on the
table anywhere . . . ? Never mind. Sit down, sit down! I
can use my empty soup-bowl. Khhghm – thpp!

My God, that's better. No, I've been sitting here all the
way through the first course just dying for one. Because I
do think it's rather bad manners to spit while one's eating.
Your mouth full of soup, and suddenly . . . khhghm –
thpp!

You *have* finished yourself, haven't you? You haven't! I'm
so sorry . . . ! Oh, you don't want the rest.

Very nice of you not to mind. One has to be so careful
these days not to offend people's prejudices. I always
ask first, of course. People never raise any objection, in
my experience. In fact they usually never say anything
at all. They generally do what you did – smile rather

charmingly and kind of wave their hand about. Quite surprised even to be asked, I think, most of them.

Khhghm . . . Where's the soup-bowl gone . . . ? No, no – sit down! Don't keep jumping up! I'll use yours! You did say you'd finished . . . ? Thpp!

I'm glad you're not one of these hysterical people who try to stop other people enjoying themselves. It's so one-sided. I don't try to stop anyone *not* spitting over me! In fact this is something I feel rather strongly about. People used to spit all the time in the good old days, and no one so much as raised an eyebrow. Spittoons everywhere you went – sawdust on the floor. Suddenly everyone went mad. Notices up in the buses – 'No Spitting. Penalty £5.' And before we knew what had happened we'd lost another of our ancient liberties.

Yes, I spit very largely as a matter of principle. And I hawk. As you can hear. Khhghm . . . ! In fact I hawk *deeply*, also as a matter of principle. Khhhhhghhhhm . . . ! Because I believe that if you're going to spit you might as well get the full benefit of it, and shift the entire contents of your lungs out into the atmosphere. Why keep all that stuff festering inside you, when you could so easily . . . Khhghm – thpp! . . . spread it around a bit . . . ?

Didn't spit in your face then, did I? I know even the most broad-minded non-spitters sometimes feel a little sensitive about getting a faceful of the stuff. I'll try to be careful – turn my head aside, and . . . Khhghm – thpp! . . . spit in your very lovely hair, or down your very charming dress.

Look, why don't I ... ? Come back, come back! I'm trying to whisper a few private words in your ear. Why don't I give you a ring some time?

We could go out and have a quiet spot of ... Khhghm – thpp! ... dinner. Or we might try something a little more exciting. I don't know. Maybe – Khhghhkhkhkhm – *thppshmk*!

You keep shaking your head. Did you get some in your ear? Don't worry – it's not as if you were inhaling it ... What's that look supposed to mean? I can't help feeling that smile of yours is beginning to get a little fixed. What – not because you got a tiny bit in your eye ... ? I did *ask*, if you remember. I did ask if you minded!

So you're one of these anti-spitting fanatics, are you? I'm not allowed to spit – is that what you're telling me? – but it's perfectly all right for you to go round leaning away from people, and grinning that ghastly glassy grin at them.

God, the *intolerance* of you lot! It makes me want to ... Well, I'll tell you what it makes me want to do. It makes me want to *khhhhhhghhhhhm* –

Oh, I can see the next course coming. I'll put that one back for later.

THEMSELVES

GAVIN OUTRIGHT And now to the serious part of the evening – the presentation of the 1997 Holdings International Personality of the Year Awards! A big hello from me, your host for the evening, Gavin Outright . . . And let's go straight on, without Further Ado, who's filming in LA and can't be with us tonight – hope you're watching, Further! – let's go straight on to the first of this evening's presentations – the J. Walter Unction Award. The J. Walter Unction Award is given annually to the person who during the past year, in the opinion of the judges, has most conspicuously succeeded in being J. Walter Unction. And here to present it, will you please welcome last year's Cheryl Upstroke Award Winner – Cheryl Upstroke!

CHERYL UPSTROKE And the J. Walter Unction Award for 1997 goes to . . .

SANDRA SMITH (*silently but glamorously hands* CHERYL UPSTROKE *an envelope.*)

[79]

CHERYL UPSTROKE Just talk among yourselves while I open the envelope . . . ! The J. Walter Unction Award for 1997 goes to – J. Walter Unction! The citation says: For being J. Walter Unction, from January 1st to December 31st, twenty-four hours a day, seven days a week, never missing a day. Not once – this is what it says here – not once was J. Walter Unction ever Trafford Lloyd Niblick or Denzil Dunning. In his unwavering devotion to being J. Walter Unction, J. Walter Unction was a shining example of consistency and perseverance to every one of us.

SANDRA SMITH (*silently but glamorously hands* CHERYL UPSTROKE *a statuette to present.*)

J. WALTER UNCTION Thank you, Cheryl. I don't know what to say. I'm gobsmacked. I really am. I just never dreamt . . . I've won this prize every year now since it was first established . . . And every year it comes as a complete and utter surprise. I'd just like to thank the judges for their faith in me, once again . . . And my parents, for . . . well, for setting up this award . . . And last but not least . . . Sorry – I'm totally overwhelmed, I'm totally choked – it happens every year . . . And last but not least – myself, for being . . . for being the person I am.

GAVIN OUTRIGHT J. Walter Unction, hot favourite for the J. Walter Unction Award, romping home once again. This is Gavin Outright, at the 1997 Holdings International Personality of the Year Awards. Coming next, right after the break, the Gavin Outright Award for the Best Gavin Outright of the Year.

(*He gazes silently into space for three minutes.*)

And welcome back to the 1997 Holdings International Personality of the Year Awards! I'm Gavin Outright, and I'm the one with butterflies myself this time because this is where we come to the Gavin Outright of the Year Award. In a year that has seen many aspirants to the title of Gavin Outright of the Year, including such outstanding contenders as Samantha Plunge, Trafford Lloyd Niblick and Cheryl Upstroke, which of them has our distinguished panel of judges picked to receive the coveted statuette? Here to present it, a man who if he's not up here winning prizes is up here presenting them – will you please welcome back J. Walter Unction Award Winner J. Walter Unction!

J. WALTER UNCTION And the Gavin Outright of the Year Award 1997 . . .

SANDRA SMITH (*silently but glamorously hands* J. WALTER UNCTION *an envelope.*)

J. WALTER UNCTION My fingers are still trembling from last time . . . The tension builds . . . Who's it going to be . . . ? The Gavin Outright of the Year Award 1997 has been won by . . . Sandra Smith! Good God! The citation says that the judges felt that it was time to welcome new blood into the industry, and to look afresh at the whole question of human identity. 'It is especially exciting,' they say, 'to see this traditionally male award going to a woman. The refreshing thing about Sandra Smith is that she completely rejects all our tired and outworn ideas of what Gavin Outright is like, and has reinterpreted his personality from the ground up in terms of her own vibrant self.' So – Sandra Smith. Who is she? Is she here?

SANDRA SMITH (*silently but glamorously hands* J. WALTER UNCTION *a statuette to present, and glamorously but loquaciously accepts it back again.*) Thank you. I just want to say that I couldn't have won this award on my own, because it takes more than one person to win anything – it takes a winner and a loser, and I want to thank Gavin Outright here for being that loser. For the judges to have awarded the Gavin Outright Award to anyone apart from Gavin Outright is a tremendous tribute to his utter nonentity. Thank you, Gavin, for being your wonderfully tired old self. Thank you for your sustained inauthenticity, for your totally committed lack of any identifiable personality. You've given a new meaning to the word selflessness. So, a sensational upset in the Gavin Outright of the Year Award! This is Sandra Smith, at the 1997 Holdings International Personality of the Year Awards. More exciting awards, right after the break – Gavin'll be fetching them, I'll be handing them out – including the hotly contested categories for Regular Attendance at Awards Ceremonies, Punctuality, and Clean Fingernails.

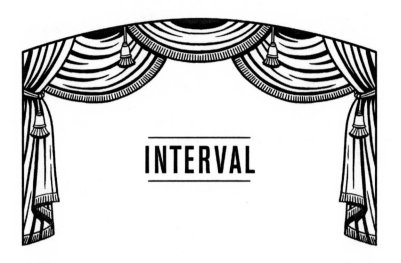

INTERVAL

Stretch our legs?

> *– Get a breath of air . . .*

Well . . . what do we think of it so far?

> *– I'm completely confused. Like, are we in a theatre, or are we in a book?*

In a book for the interval, at any rate. We might manage to get a drink for once if it's our own drink. Small white wine?

> *– And a few nuts, perhaps. Also there's no queue for the Ladies'.*

So, we're in a book.

> *– For the moment. Or a theatre, of course. Or neither. Or both. It's that kind of thing.*

You mean sort of, what's reality and what's not? Sort of, is everything in the world actually inside our heads?

    – *Are we really here ourselves or are we just figments of the imagination?*

And if so who figged us? Pretty deep stuff.

    – *The couple in some of those items . . . They weren't supposed to be you and me, were they, by any chance?*

Probably. Getting in a bit of a dig at the customers. Putting us all down. Grab the money and then kick you on the kneecaps. Do you feel suitably got at?

    – *Totally annihilated. If I was ever here in the first place.*

Have you got the programme? How much more of this have we got to sit through?

    – *Let's see . . . Oh, my God, another fifteen items!*

We could do a bunk. What do you think?

    – *Not go back in for the second half?*

Leisurely dinner. Early night.

    – *Well . . . Better stick it out, perhaps, now we've got this far.*

What, England expects, kind of thing?

[84]

– Try to get our money's worth.

Grit our teeth.

– We should be getting back. Wasn't that the bell?

I didn't hear anything. Inside your head, perhaps.

– Like everything else. Possibly.

Your head probably being inside my *head.*

– Which I expect is inside mine.

Take our drinks back in with us, anyway. Have we got a couple of plastic cups?

– Bring the glasses! No one's going to notice!

MEMORIAL

LEONARD LEADER Hello, my name's Leonard Leader, and I'm the Senior Spiritual Affairs Consultant at this theatre. I'd like to wish you all a very warm welcome to the second half of our programme tonight.

But first – and there's always a 'But first' on these occasions, isn't there! – but first, let us take a few moments to share our thoughts and memories of something that I think was very dear to all of us here. Let us pause to remember the interval. To give thanks for that particular span of time that so very recently drew to a close, and that remains so very fresh in all our minds.

This is not a sad occasion but a happy one. We have come together here, in this beautiful theatre, not to mourn but to celebrate. It's true that the interval is over, its life is finished, and that fact, of course, is something that we all have to come to terms with. But we've all said our goodbyes already. This is not a funeral. It is a service of memorial, an act of rejoicing and thanks-giving.

I think all of us here loved that interval. We all have many happy memories of it. It brought so much joy into all our lives.

And yet it lasted for so short a time. Can it be true that it was with us for only twenty minutes? We look back over those twenty minutes, and how crowded they seem! How fortunate we feel ourselves to have known it, to have been blessed and enriched by it!

It was a time for stretching our legs. A time for getting a breath of air, and recharging our batteries. A time, perhaps, for talking to our friends. Or perhaps simply for quiet reflection – for meditation on the show so far, for preparing ourselves for what is yet to come.

The end of that interval for all of us marks in some sense the end of an epoch. There will, surely, never be an interval quite like it again.

What *was* it like, this interval we knew so well? What did it mean to us all as individuals? First, a personal recollec-tion by Mrs Hilda Trumble.

HILDA TRUMBLE In some ways it was an interval just like any other interval. I think that this is what was so special about it. I remember when I first made its acquaintance. I'd been sitting in Row C, and I began to realise that something had changed in my life. I was not as untroubled and serene within myself as I once had been. There was a journey I had to make, a quest I had to attempt. Well, I was pretty solidly stuck in my life down there in Row C, and if the interval hadn't come along I don't believe I could have managed to make the break. And if I hadn't – I hate to think what might have become of me. I wonder how many other people there are here who are just that little bit more comfortable with themselves thanks to the interval? Of course, we tend to take these things entirely for granted at the time, and sometimes we find we haven't made full use of our opportunities before they are suddenly snatched away. My one regret is that I didn't also seize the chance to have a small glass of white wine.

GEORGE GRICE George Grice, Row G. For me this interval was quite unique. Things happened during it that have never happened in any of the many other intervals I have known. I will give you just one example of this. It was during the interval that my wife remembered that she had forgotten to set the oven before we came out this evening, as we had specifically agreed, so that the chicken casserole I had prepared would not in fact be cooked. If it had not been for the interval she might not have realised until we had got home, and we should both have missed a great deal to talk about, and to reflect on in the second half.

WENDY WILDE I just want to say it was a lovely interval – oh, I'm Wendy Wilde, in Row J – and I don't know anything about intervals, but I loved it, and I think everyone loved it, and you could just tell it was trying to make everyone happy, because as soon as it started I found this shoe under my seat, and I couldn't think how it had got there, I mean I sometimes take my shoes off in strange places, but this was a man's shoe, and then I saw that there was this man two rows behind looking very embarrassed, and he's called Cedric, and he's in alternative therapy, and he's a Capricorn, and we're going to have coffee afterwards, and I just want to say, 'Thank you, interval!'

LEONARD LEADER Before we return to our busy lives, let us take a moment to offer up our thanks to the management of this theatre, who give intervals and who take them away. And let us keep the memory of this interval bright by dedicating ourselves to being perhaps just that little bit more alert and appreciative in the second half. And let us remember, if our hearts be weary, that a time will surely come hereafter when we and the interval are reunited. Only this time it will abide with us not for twenty minutes, but forever. And now, with the strains of some suitably profound but joyous music ringing in our ears, let us go bravely forth into the battle once again.

BING BONG!

An airport departure lounge. Two anguished lovers. One public address system.

PUBLIC ADDRESS SYSTEM: *Bing bong!*

This is the final call for passengers on Flight DB 473 to Bucharest. Will any remaining passengers for this flight go at once to Gate 47, where the flight is now closing.

Bing bong!

Flight GK 279 to Ankara is now ready for boarding through Gate 51.

SHE: Helsinki? Was that Helsinki? Did they say Helsinki?

HE: No, no. Somewhere.
Not Helsinki.

SHE: It wasn't *your* flight? It
wasn't Birmingham?

HE: It was Amsterdam or
Malaga or somewhere. It
wasn't Birmingham.

*Bing bong! We regret to
announce the further delay
to delayed Flight KL 319 to
Dubai. Will all passengers
for this flight please listen for
further announcements.*

SHE: I can't bear this! I don't
know what they're saying!
I don't know what I'm
doing . . . !

HE: Oh, darling!

SHE: You're going to be back
in Birmingham, and I'm
going to be back in Helsinki,
and we're never going to see
each other again!

HE: We'll think of each
other. We'll go on thinking
of each other.

SHE: But we'll never be able
to talk to each other! Never,
never again!

HE: All the things I want to say to you!

SHE: And any moment they're going to be calling our flights.

HE: Our last chance to talk! Forever and ever!

Bing bong!

SHE: Oh, no!

Passengers are reminded that smoking is not permitted in any part of the airport buildings.

HE: All right. We've another moment. Listen, darling, listen. Before they *do* call them. These last few days for me weren't just . . .

Bing bong!

SHE: Listen, listen!

Flight TT 222 to Timbuctoo is now ready for boarding through Gate 8.

Sorry! Sorry! I thought it might be our flights.

HE: No, I was just saying that for me these last few days weren't just . . .

Bing bong!

. . . you know, they weren't just . . .

[92]

... a passing moment of ~~madness — Well, they were~~ ~~madness, yes, but a kind~~ ~~of madness I've never felt~~ ~~anything like before ...~~

For security reasons please ensure that luggage and other personal items are not left unattended at any time. Unattended items may be removed and destroyed.

SHE: Oh, darling!

HE: Have you?

SHE: Yes!

HE: Yes?

SHE: Yes, yes!

HE: You *have* felt something like this before?

SHE: Yes! No! No!

HE: You didn't hear what I said?

SHE: Yes! No! No!

HE: I said ...

Bing bong!

I said ...

~~I've never felt anything~~ ~~like this in my entire life~~ ~~before ...~~

Flight JK 453 to Helsinki is now ready for boarding through Gate 73.

SHE: What?

HE: I've never ...

[93]

SHE: Never . . . ?

HE: Felt anything . . .

SHE: You didn't . . . ?

. . . feel anything?

HE: Like this! Before!

Oh . . . !
~~Like what I'm feeling now!~~
~~Never! Never in my life!~~
~~Never felt anything . . .~~

. . . like this. Before. Never. Never before. Like this. Never felt. Before.

SHE: Oh, darling! You remember when we stood looking out over the lake in the moonlight that night, and you said . . .

HE: And I said . . . ?

SHE: ~~. . . if only this moment could go on. On and on and on until the end of time, forever and forever and forever . . .~~

Bing bong!

This is the final call for Flight GK 279 to Ankara. Will all remaining passengers for this flight go immediately to Gate 51.

Bing bong!

Flight TR 399 for Birmingham is now ready for boarding through Gate 41.

Bing bong!

As a courtesy to other passengers please ensure that your voice is kept down at all times when making personal conversation.

[94]

. . . and forever.

HE: Forever?

SHE: Forever! Yes!

HE: You'll love me?

SHE: No!

HE: No?

SHE: Yes! No! This moment!

HE: This moment?

SHE: That moment!

HE: That moment? What moment? Which moment?

SHE: By the lake! In the moonlight! Go on forever! What you said!

Bing bong!

You said . . .
~~. . . if only this moment could go on and on until the end of time, forever and forever and forever . . .~~

Passengers are reminded that weeping is not permitted in any part of the airport buildings, and laughing is permitted only in the designated laughing areas.

HE: I said . . . ? *What* did I say . . . ?

SHE: It doesn't matter . . . Oh, darling!

[95]

HE: Oh, darling! If only we could spend the rest of our lives together.

SHE: But I know you have to . . .

Bing bong!

Passengers are reminded that no talking is permitted while this announcement is being made.

~~. . . go back to your family in Birmingham, and you know I'd never do anything that would come between you and them . . .~~

And you do understand, I know, that . . .

Bing bong!

This is a security announcement. Please ensure that you are aware of this fact.

~~. . . that my life's in Helsinki – I have family, too . . .~~

You do understand that, don't you, darling?

HE: Yes! You mean – that you love me?

SHE: No, no, no.

HE: You *don't* love me?

SHE: Yes! Yes! But what I said was . . .

Bing bong!

What I said was . . .
~~. . . I have a life, too, I have elderly parents I could never just walk out on.~~

This is the final call for passengers on Flight JK 453 to Helsinki.

HE: I do understand, darling.

SHE: ~~My aunt is bedridden, she depends on me ... I have two dogs ... A cat ...~~ *Will all remaining passengers for this flight go at once to Gate 73, where the flight is now closing.*

HE: I know. I know.

SHE: They still haven't called our flights ... Unless they have, and we didn't hear it ...

HE: Did I tell you ...

Did I tell you ... *Bing bong!*

~~... how I love it when you make that funny little anxious face of yours?~~ *This is the final call for passengers on Flight TR 399 for Birmingham.*

SHE: Tell me what?

HE: Tell you ...
~~... how I love it when you make that funny little anxious face of yours?~~ *Will all remaining passengers for this flight go at once to Gate 41, where the flight is now closing.*

SHE: You mean ... by the lake?

HE: By the lake?

SHE: Tell me. By the lake. Did you?

HE: Yes, or ever?

[97]

SHE: Ever?

HE: Ever. Ever tell you.

SHE: Yes . . . No . . . Tell me
what?

HE: How I love it when
you . . .

When you . . .
~~. . . make that face . . . that
face . . . that face . . . !~~

Bing bong!

*Please be aware that no an-
nouncements have been made
now for nearly fifteen seconds.*

SHE: I'm sorry – I can't bear
this! I'm going to say . . .

Bing bong!

Goodbye!

HE: Goodbye?

SHE: ~~I'm going to say
goodbye now, because I
just can't bear sharing this
conversation with a loud-
speaker.~~

*Please listen carefully for
further announcements, as no
further announcements will be
made.*

You do understand, darling?

HE: Goodbye? Just . . . goodbye?

SHE: Say it. Going to. Going
to say it now. Because I can't
bear trying to share this
conversation with a . . .

[98]

Bing bong!

. . . with a loudspeaker!

~~But then I can't bear to say goodbye . . . I don't know what I'm doing . . . I'm going crazy . . . !~~

Please be aware that passengers who insist on talking to each other instead of listening to these announcements do so at their own risk.

HE: Wait! Listen!

Bing bong!

Listen, listen!

~~We can't say goodbye! All I want to do is to spend the rest of my life with you!~~

Because what do you think it's like for me doing this? Do you think I like talking to myself?

SHE: Me? Is that me?

HE: You! Yes! Yes! You!

SHE: Oh no! No, no, no!

HE: No?

SHE: Helsinki?

HE: Helsinki?

SHE: You said they said Helsinki?

HE: No, no, no. Listen, listen! Don't go! Phone your husband. Now! Tell him . . .

Bing bong!

Tell him . . .

~~. . . the simple truth. I know it will be hard – hard for him, and hard for you – but sometimes in life one has to face up to the truth however hard it is . . .~~

Can you hear what I'm saying? What do you think I feel, being left out in the cold while you two conduct your squalid little affair under my nose?

That wasn't Birmingham?

SHE: No! Yes! No! Don't leave me!

HE: You mean . . .

I mean, use your imagination!

. . . you *will* . . .

~~. . . phone him? You will tell him? Even though it's going to hurt him – and I know you love him and you don't want to hurt him?~~

Don't you think I feel lonely and jealous? Don't you think I'd like to find another loudspeaker to have little secret conversations with?

SHE: Yes!

HE: Yes?

SHE: Forever!

HE: Forever? You do understand what I'm saying?

SHE: I understand what you're saying, darling. And you understand . . .

Bing bong!

. . . that I love . . .

~~... the way you understand everything I say. And I will think of you, my darling.~~

Don't you think the two of us would have been on the first flight going anywhere out of here together?

I will! I will!

HE: You will?

SHE: Of course I will!

HE: Spend the rest of your life with me?

SHE: Spend the ... what? No – think of you, think of you!

HE: Just a moment. We've got a crossed line here. Are we or aren't we ... ?

Bing bong!

Wait, wait. This is very important.

I'm not getting through to you, am I? All right, if that's how you want to be.

Now! Quick! Before it starts again. Are we or aren't we ... ?

Bing bong!

SHE: Are we or aren't we ... ?

HE: Wait.

This is a final call for Passenger Porton on Flight GBH 4098 to Helsinki.

[101]

SHE: Never going to see each other again?

HE: Going to spend the rest of our lives together?

Also for Passenger Cuthbertson on Flight RIP 4713 to Birmingham.

SHE: What?

HE: What?

Will Passengers Porton and Cuthbertson please go to their gates immediately.

SHE: Spend the rest of our lives together?

HE: Never see each other again?

SHE: ~~No, no, no! Listen, listen, listen!~~

HE: ~~Listen, listen, listen! No, no, no!~~

And when Passengers Porton and Cuthbertson do finally stop talking to each other and listen to what I'm saying . . .

. . . they're going to get the shock of their lives, are Passengers Porton and Cuthbertson, because their flights will have gone.

SHE: *What* did they say?

Oh, so now you're listening! Too late, my loves – I'm not going to repeat it. You'll just have to stay behind after everybody else has gone and go through the whole agonising performance again with the next flight.

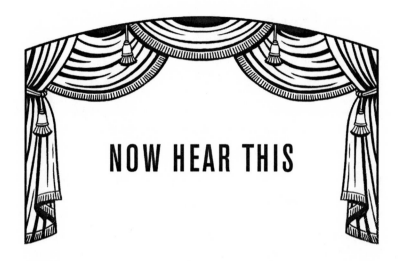

NOW HEAR THIS

That drain outside the back door's blocked again.

   – Oh dear.

The drain! It's blocked again!

   – Oh good.

You'll have to do something about it.

   – Right, right.

Did you hear what I said?

   – Of course.

You didn't, did you!

– Didn't I?

*

Right, a new chapter in the conversation.

   – Right.

It often puzzles me.

   – I imagine so.

You never listen to anything I say. But you often know I'm saying something.

   – Often, yes.

And you know I've come to the end of saying it.

   – Well, these things happen.

You know you're then supposed to say something in return.

   – Something, yes.

'Something.' Exactly. So you must have been aware that words were being said.

   – Was I?

You just haven't understood them.

– Of course not.

So that what we're saying has the grammatical shape of a conversation.

– Oh, I think so.

Without actually being a conversation.

– I suppose not.

But if you haven't understood what I've said, I don't know how you decide what to reply.

– Don't you?

Whether it's 'Don't you?' or 'I suppose so' or 'Right.'

– Right.

*

That was a pause while I was thinking about the problem. It seems to me you must at any rate take in my tone of voice. You must hear, for instance, whether it's positive or negative.

– I expect so.

Which I appreciate.

– Not at all.

So, let me try saying something negative in a positive voice, and vice versa . . . Wonderful news, dear! Your old friend Peter Plaster has died!

– Oh, good.

But I'm afraid he's left you half a million pounds in his will.

– Oh dear.

*

As a matter of fact he hasn't died. Peter Plaster. Your old friend. In fact I saw him yesterday. We had lunch together. It was a very strange experience.

– I suppose it must have been.

Because he actually seemed to be listening to what I was saying. He actually said things himself.

– Well, there you are.

Such as that he's going away to work in Romania, and he wants me to go with him.

– Does he?

Perhaps I should.

– Perhaps.

*

That last exchange. That's a rather good example of what I mean. It made perfectly good syntactical sense. 'He wants me to go with him.' – 'Does he?' – 'Perhaps I should.' – 'Perhaps.' I find that quite reassuring.

   – Good.

Where things go completely off the rails is if I'm stupid enough to ask you a question that requires some actual substantive response, some original input.

   – That's right.

Such as, 'What is the capital of Romania?'

   – That's true.

You see?

   – Yes, quite . . . So did you?

So did I? Good God! A question! You asked me a question! You made some contribution! Did I something. Did I what?

   – Go off with whoever it was. Don't you ever listen
     to anything you say?

*

No, I didn't. Go off with whoever it was. As you

might have noticed. Because here I am, talking to you. Remember?

    – I suppose so . . . Bucharest, incidentally.

Bucharest?

    – The capital of Romania.

A STIFF DRINK

You know who I am?

   – Yes.

Who am I?

   – My interrogator.

Your interrogator, yes. That is a very frank answer. It is a hopeful beginning to our conversation.

   – Thank you.

Your identification of me suggests a shrewd and well-informed mind.

   – Kind of you to say so.

You were not deceived by my jovial manner?

– No.

You know that interrogators often have a jovial manner?

– Yes.

It makes them, paradoxically, even more sinister.

– Much more.

Which is required by the nature of the work.

– I understand that.

You have seen interrogators going about their business before?

– Yes.

In plays?

– Yes.

I wrote those plays.

– Oh.

I am, in some sense, the author of this one. Perhaps.

– Ah.

I embody certain aspects of the author. Possibly. It is not certain. The question is left open.

– I understand.

The author is himself a jovial man. It has often been remarked upon.

– Yes.

In his case, too, however, the truth may be more complex.

– I'm sure it is.

I am pouring myself a stiff drink.

– Yes.

This may suggest to you a brutal and terrifying disregard of the niceties of interrogation.

– Not at all.

On the other hand it may indicate that I suffer some underlying unease about my work. A need to blunt my sensibilities.

– Hardly.

In any case, your opinion on the matter is of no interest.

– Of course not.

Your part in these proceedings is to be my victim.

– I understand that.

It is a modest part.

– Of course.

But not without its importance.

– Thank you.

You may represent another aspect of the author. Some more passive side to his nature. A vulnerability that he has endeavoured to conceal from the world.

– Possibly.

Though you seem to have remarkably little to say for yourself.

– Remarkably little.

Do I detect a note of reproach in your voice?

– No.

You should be glad to have any words at all.

– I am.

You may have found this dialogue sparse on the page.

– Not at all.

But now you see it performed, by a well-known actor, you understand the depths of meaning that lie beneath it.

– I do.

We are talking about my part.

– I realise.

It is an important part.

– Highly important.

It is a part that I may possibly be persuaded to take myself in some future production. If it can be fitted in with my other commitments.

– I look forward to seeing that.

The case with your part is somewhat different. It has unfortunately not proved possible to secure a leading actor to play it.

– I'm sorry.

A leading actor would feel that you have too little to say.

– I understand.

He would object that your character does not develop in any very interesting or dramatic way.

– He would be right.

You are entirely passive.

– I am.

A pathetic creature.

– Hopeless.

But this is because of the nature of the play in which you are appearing.

– Of course.

It is not the sort of play in which the victim bravely defies his tormentor. It is not that sort of play at all. There are different sorts of play. This is a simple play. A painful play. An important but short play. A play without a plot. In this respect it is like life.

– Like my life.

Like your life. Yes. Not like my life. That is true. My life has a plot. You sighed.

– It was in the stage directions.

Were you sighing at the depths of human cruelty revealed by the play?

– I believe I was.

You were not sighing at the play itself?

– No.

I am relieved to hear it. Our conversation might have taken a less friendly turn. Look on the bright side. You might have had no words at all. You might have been a wordless shadowy presence, indicating your humanity and your suffering with nothing more than a bowed head.

 – I realise that.

Though a good supporting or character actor can do a great deal with silence and a bowed head.

 – On second thoughts you might wish to consider taking the part yourself.

If I should require artistic advice I will extract it by torture. Do you know how long this little conversation of ours has been going on?

 – A long time.

Four and three-quarter minutes. You understand now that torture is wrong?

 – I understand that now.

You did not understand that simple moral point before?

 – Apparently not.

You are a moral cretin.

 – So I realise.

The torment will continue for another twenty-three seconds. Then it will stop.

    – Thank you. Thank you!

You at last show signs of animation. Something has perhaps been achieved by this little conversation of ours.

    – I believe it has.

You may silently count the seconds remaining if you wish. There are seven of them.

(*A pause lasting seven seconds. Curtain.*)

PRECISELY SO

Speaking as one mathematician to another . . .

– Hold on. Speaking as *exactly* one mathematician?

Well – to a first approximation.

– And speaking to a similar approximation of another mathematician?

Let's say to within ± 0.001 of a mathematician in both cases.

– So allowing for incremental error, we are talking about a conversation involving something between 1.998 and 2.002 mathematicians altogether?

Correct. To three places of decimals. Anyway, if I might have a word.

– Just one?

Well, more accurately, perhaps, a series $\{a_n\}$ of words, where the value of n has yet to be assigned.

– But it can be assumed to be a positive number?

A positive real whole number, certainly. Is it a good moment?

– 18.27:31 GMT would be good for me. Is 18.27:31 GMT good for you?

Could we make it more like 18.27:47? I'm hoping to fit a small sneeze in at around 18.27:33.

– Of course. So ... 18.27:45 ... 18.27:46 ... And off you go.

Thank you. Well, it's a slightly awkward personal matter. You know of course that ψ has had this terrible falling out with θ?

– I know ψ told θ that $D = \min_{1 \le i \le n} \left\{ \min_{1 \le j \le n, i \ne j} \left\{ \frac{d(i,j)}{\max_{1 \le k \le n} d'(k)} \right\} \right\}$

Yes, well, now θ has complained to her sister that $DB = \frac{1}{n} \sum_{i=1}^{n} \max_{i \ne j} \left(\frac{\sigma_i + \sigma_j}{d(c_i, c_j)} \right)$

– Oh, no! But is that really true? For all values of D and d?

I'm absolutely +.

– Positive? Are you? It sounds such a negative view of things! And positive x negative = negative.

Exactly! Which makes two negatives, and negative x negative = positive. Anyway, now something $\geq$ has happened.

– Heavens above! Something equal to or greater than that?

Yesterday evening just as $N(\psi_y, \mu_y)$, there was a shot, and . . . well . . . in a word, $X_{t+s} - X_t = \int_t^{t+s} \mu(X_u, u)\mathrm{d}u + \int_t^{t+s} \sigma(X_u, u)\mathrm{d}B_u$.

– Oh my God!

ψ got so angry! '$\sqrt{\eta_{mq}}$!' he shouted. 'Σ max $(q + q^{gg})^2 \approx 0$!!!'

– That is surely racially abusive mathematics!

So then of course things became really ugly. It's difficult to believe this, but within minutes $\frac{\delta f(x,t)}{\delta t} = -\sum_{i=1}^{N} \frac{\delta}{\delta x_i} [\mu_i(x)f(x,t)] + \sum_{i=1}^{N} \sum_{j=1}^{N} \frac{\delta^2}{\delta x_i \delta x_j} [D_{ij}(x)f(x,t)]$.

– The trouble is that ψ is so stochastic.

Anyway, if you could have a quiet figure or two with him.

– I'll drop him a line.

If you would. At right angles to the horizontal.

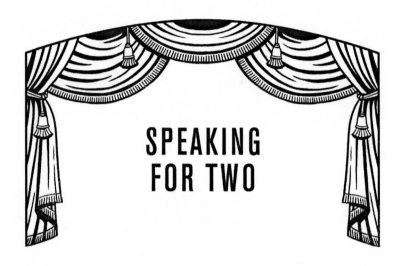

SPEAKING FOR TWO

So, are we going to the Nodgets' on the seventeenth or aren't we?

   – Oh . . .

And don't say 'Let's think about it.'

   – No . . .

Or 'It depends,' because it doesn't depend, we just have to decide.

   – Yes, only . . .

Or 'Yes, only.' Or 'What do *you* think?', because I know what *I* think, I just want to know what *you* think.

   – All right . . .

'All right'? You mean 'All right, we'll go'?

   – No . . .

No, of course not. You mean 'All right, we'll think about it.' But it's *not* all right, because you *won't* think about it, you never do unless I keep on at you.

   – No, only . . .

And here we go again! 'Yes only, no only . . . If . . . But . . . Well . . .' All I need you to say is simply 'yes' or 'no', but of course there's always some reason why you can't, because . . .

   – Yes, because . . .

Exactly, 'because! Because, because, because!'

   – Because . . .

And all you can do is interrupt me!

   – No, but . . .

I've only got to open my mouth, and yet again, before I can say two words, you've interrupted me!

   – I didn't . . . I wasn't . . .

Yes, you did! And next thing we know . . .

   – Listen . . .

There you go *again*!

– No . . .

And again! And now of course you're not just interrupting
me . . .

– No, I'm . . .

. . . you're contradicting everything I say!

– Well . . .

'Well.' You see? I can never utter so much as a single
word without your immediately saying the opposite! I
say 'yes' – you say 'no'.

– I didn't . . .

I say you did – you say you didn't!

– I wasn't . . .

I say you were – you say you weren't! You *were* contradicting me!

– I was just . . .

And there you go again! Every word I say! Some demon
gets into you!

– I wasn't . . .

Just listen to yourself!

– I can't . . .

Can't listen to yourself, no, of course you can't! You can't
hear a word you're saying because you're too busy pick-
ing on *me*! If you just listened for once, instead of perpet-
ually interrupting and contradicting, you might actually
hear what you're saying!

– Well . . .

And at once of course you flare up! You won't accept
a word of criticism . . . ! Will you? I said, 'Will you?'
Oh, silence now. Didn't you hear what I said? Or am I
talking to myself . . . ? You're always doing this! Refusing
to say anything . . . ! Just silently sighing to yourself and
thinking I can't hear it. You might as well sigh out loud
and make a meal of it, because I know you're still contradicting me.

– Yes.

'Yes'? Oh. What's this? All of a sudden you're agreeing
with me?

– No . . .

And of course as soon as I say you're agreeing you say
you're not!

– No, I mean Yes, we won't go to the Nodgets'.

TWELFTH NIGHT, OR IF YOU LIKE, TIMON OF ATHENS

So what I'm proposing to attempt in this talk is, if you like, an *investigation* into why anyone who makes any kind of, if you like, *comment* on anything these days has to stress so many of the words as if they were in a foreign language, and then put 'if you like' in front of them. I suspect that it's intended to suggest some kind of . . .

   – Hold on a moment. If I like?

. . . some kind of, if you like, *flexibility* and *open-mindedness.* Some kind of, if you like, *interactive role* for the audience. Which is what people have come to expect because of endlessly being invited to post their own comments on whatever they read on the internet . . .

   – Hold on, hold on! If I like?

Who is this?

– Me. Out here. I'm waving my arms.

Oh, you. Right. And who, if I may ask, might you be?

– I'm 'you'.

You're me?

– No, I'm 'you'. You said 'if you like'. That's me. 'You' is me.

Yes, well, when I say 'you' it doesn't mean *you*.

– When you say 'you' it doesn't mean 'you'?

Not you *personally*. It means, if you like, *one*.

– One? *If I like*, one? I *am* one! Look! Do you see two of me standing here? Or three of me? No, there's one of me! Whether I like it or not!

Exactly! There's only one of you! You can't be 'one' if there's only one of you! 'One' doesn't mean one!

– 'One' doesn't mean one?

Not just one single person! It means all sorts of people! Him, her, them . . . *Me*, if you like.

– You?

If you like.

– If I like? So, *if I like*, when you say it's, if you like, *bendability* or whatever it was, you mean it's bend-ability if *you* like? And don't say 'if you like' again, because I *don't* like!

You *don't* like? You mean you don't like my having just as much right to be consulted about what I like or don't like as you have?

– I don't like your telling me you'll call something something if *I* like and then finding out it means if *you* like.

Fair enough. So what *would* you like?

– Me? Oh, a cup of tea – milk, no sugar – and an Eccles cake. Thank you. How about you?

Early retirement and a small house in the Lot-et-Garonne.

– So on this point we, if you like, *agree to differ*?

If you like.

– Then press the, if you like, *little button* that says 'like'.

BLACKOUT NUMBER

When the actors leave the stage at the end of a scene, and darkness falls on our brightly-lit familiar world, another world comes to life. The secret world of the *sceneshifters*.

Somewhere in the darkness a little head pops out of its hole. Then another . . . and another . . . They sniff the air, checking that it's safe to leave their burrows.

And out from their holes all round the stage emerge perhaps the most remarkable of all nocturnal creatures. You may sometimes have caught brief glimpses of them as they scurried about their business in the darkness, but now for the first time we can see their fascinating habits in detail, thanks to the magic of infra-red light.

Sceneshifters are primates, members of the same genus as ourselves, but Nature has endowed them with various skills that we don't have. The most obvious is their uncanny ability to see in the dark, which enables them to scuttle around in these amazingly complicated patterns without ever bumping into each other.

They may look to us as if they're playing some elaborate game, but in fact everything that these little creatures do has a serious purpose. In the few short moments of darkness at their disposal they must hunt out the food and drink they need to keep themselves alive through the next scene. Most of all they love the half-eaten remains of mashed banana, and the dregs of cold tea or blackcurrant cordial at the bottom of a wine glass. Books are another delicacy. A fully-grown sceneshifter can eat his bodyweight of assorted paperbacks in the course of a single act.

While some are searching for food, others are rooting out nest-building materials – odd sticks of furniture and scraps of scenery abandoned by the departing actors. The sceneshifters will hide these away inside their burrows, and weave them together to make the nests where they sleep while the rest of the world is awake. This young male is struggling with a piece of scenery bigger than he is . . . Will it go into the hole this way . . . ? No . . . That way . . . ?

Sceneshifters are as clean in their habits as cats, and before the light returns they will have cleared out all their old nest material and arranged it neatly about the stage in complex patterns that serve a rather surprising purpose. The most fascinating thing of all about these denizens of the night is that they have a symbiotic rela-tionship with their natural enemies, the actors. Actors depend upon finding fresh supplies of old nest material when they return, placed in certain very exact positions. Without them they would have nothing to sit on, or to drink at moments of stress, or to throw at each other in their characteristic mating rituals.

How do the sceneshifters know where everything goes? What is the concealed code that makes it possible? The secret lies in those little pieces of gaffer tape stuck to the floor, almost invisible to the human eye.

Watch these three as they all work together to move a large object like a table . . . They not only have to be able to see the little pieces of tape in the dark – they have to remember, out of all the hundreds of little pieces of tape on the floor, which are which. Is this the mark for the table or the chair? *She* seems to think it's the mark for the table – but in the scene before last. *He* evidently thinks it's where the sideboard goes in the next scene . . . How they manage to communicate all this to each other is not fully understood, but it seems to involve a language of little squeaks too high for the human ear to hear.

Now watch . . . They're snuffing the air again. They've sensed danger. They know that soon it will begin to get light, and woe betide any sceneshifter caught by the actors on their territory.

And away they all scuttle into their holes . . . The little one's running back . . . She's dropped something . . . She's in danger of being caught and eaten alive . . . No, here comes the mother sceneshifter to chivvy her off . . .

And once again the nightly miracle of the scene change is completed just in time for . . .

. . . the next scene.

WE HAVE BEEN HERE BEFORE

We should have gone left.

   – What?

At that last fork. We went right. We should have gone left.

   – So why didn't you say? We've driven past it now!

Sorry – I've only just realised. Stop, stop. Turn round. Here, look. Through the forecourt of this petrol station.

   – This is what we did last year. It's all coming back to me.

Exactly. We should have gone left last year, only we didn't, we went right, and it was wrong.

   – No, actually – now I remember! – we didn't go

right last year. We went left. And it was wrong, and we had to turn round and go back, and go right.

No, last year we should have gone left. Only we didn't. We went right. Now we've done it again.

   – Yes, and I know why I turned right. Because it's right. It's actually very easy to remember. Right's right.

No, what we agreed to remember last year was that right's wrong.

   – 'Right's wrong'? That's a rather striking proposition. I think I'd remember if we'd said 'Right's wrong.'

Exactly. Exactly! You would remember! We'd both remember! That's why we kept saying it. 'Right's wrong! Right's wrong!' And we turned round at this same petrol station.

   – At this same petrol station, yes. Only that wasn't last year, it was the year before last. We went right, and we turned round at this petrol station. Because you said we should have gone left, so we went back and went left, and of course it was wrong, so we had to turn round yet again and come back, and go right.

You're thinking of the other petrol station.

   – What other petrol station?

The one on the other road, after we'd turned left, and you said it was wrong, and you insisted we went back and went right, only this was wrong, so then, yes, it's true – we did turn round at this petrol station, and went back and turned left.

– It's funny, isn't it. Every year we go to the same place . . .

We try to go to the same place.

– . . . and every year we go backwards and forwards saying we should have gone left, we should have gone right, this petrol station, that petrol station . . .

. . . and every year we end up going right, which we shouldn't do, year after year, if right wasn't right . . .

– So let's get it absolutely straight in our minds for next year. We go right and it's wrong . . .

We go right and we think it's wrong, so we turn round and we go right, because left's right if you're going in the opposite direction . . .

– So now right's wrong, and we turn round and go left, because right's now left . . . No . . . Yes . . .

Right!

– Right. We're agreed.

No – turn right! Here! Right, right, right . . . ! And of

course you've missed it! Again! You missed it when we went back last year!

– And the year before.

So here's the other petrol station where we always turn . . .

OTTER STRIKE

Hi! Great to see you again! So, you're out of bed! You're on the mend! Wonderful! And looking fit as a fiddle! Though I gather there are still one or two problems . . .

– Ritchie soak foursome rider.

Right, right . . . Don't worry, anyway. I can't understand a word my wife says, either! She can't understand a word I say! I'll just put in plenty of exclamation marks! I won't ask any questions! So . . . How are things?

– Strawdle bawdle. Foodle doodle.

That sounds good.

– Indle ordle wardle warble.

Yes . . . Yes . . .

– Tish tush stringbuddy.

'Stringbuddy'? Wonderful! Well done!

– Ishkosh too too dinkrush.

Oh, I'm sorry to hear that.

– Blue, blue, blue! Ishkosh!

Ishkosh, right.

– Ishkosh too also dinkrush!

Too also . . . ?

– Dinkrush!

Dinkrush. Exactly. Exactly . . .

*

Well, at least the weather's nice! And you've got a bit of a view out of the window here!

– Dorsal . . . Tish tosh, ma dorsal . . .

Wonderful. Great. Dinkrush, in fact!

– Tosh dinkrush!

Tosh dinkrush? Right. Not so dinkrush!

– Tosh tosh tosh dinkrush! Weewee tootle!

OK. I see that. Yes . . . Yes . . . I see that . . .

*

So . . . let's think . . . What's been happening in the great outside world? Not a lot! What have I seen on television recently?

   – [*Oh, no! Not television!*]

I can't remember . . .

   – [*Dementia already? How sad.*]

I read a rather interesting book, though. What was it called . . . ?

   – [*I'll go mad if I have to sit here and listen to this nonsense much longer. Why doesn't he go away and leave me to talk to myself? It's all perfectly clear in here, inside my head!*]

What?

   – [*What does he mean, 'What?'?*]

You were pointing to your head. What – a headache? I'll find an aspirin . . .

   – Spod, spod!

No? OK . . . Something to do with your hair . . . You want a comb? A hairbrush?

– Spick! Span!

A haircut? A head massage? Psychoanalysis . . . ? Hold on – what's this . . . ? This gesture you're making . . . Turn the heating down?

– ['*Turn the heating down*'! *Oh, for God's sake! It means calm down! Obviously! It means relax! It means stop trying too hard!*]

No? OK, so – turn the heating *up* . . . ? Get down on the floor . . . ? Look under the bed . . . ? Hold on . . . Your mouth. You're pointing to your mouth. Something about your mouth . . .

– [*Yes! Don't put words into it!*]

Something to eat? To drink . . . ?

– [*Oh, come on!*] Dordle ordle spod spod spod!

A cup of tea. You want a cup of tea. Of course. Milk, no sugar . . . ?

– Ha! Ha!

So, not tea . . . Toothbrush? A sore throat?

– Ha! Ha! Ha! Ha!

False teeth? Be sick?

– Na! Na!

Na?

– Ha!

Ha, yes. Or na . . .

– [*Just as well, perhaps, that he doesn't know what's going on in here. He might take it very much amiss.*]

*

So, there we are, then. There we are . . . Oh, my God, look at the time . . . ! I must be going.

– [*Oh, must you? You've only been here about two minutes. Though it seems more like two hours, I agree.*]

Yes . . . I really must be off . . .

– [*Go on, then . . . Why are you still sitting here? Can't you even guess what I'm feeling? You can't, can you! We're living in different universes!*]

Oh, I know . . . I saw Mrs Brodbag the other day. You remember Mrs Brodbag . . . ?

– [*Oh, no! Not Mrs Brodbag! This really is scraping the barrel! I'll have to tell him in so many words.*] Schnort pistachio plodhouse!

Yes – wonderful woman. Anyway . . .

   – Schnort plodhouse! Pistachio plodhouse!

No, rather terrible woman, I agree.

   – Scurt maltravers treadwater!

Oh, yes – married to your cousin. Of course. I'm so sorry.

   – Treadwater treadwater treadwater!

She did indeed. She still does.

   – Strayforth tawdry tick tick!

Right.

   – [*How can I put that politely?*] Norse fall otter strike!

OK. Norse fall . . . ?

   – Otter strike!

OK.

   – Na?

Ya. Yes.

   – [*Go on, then! Go!*] Plum! Plum, plum, plum! Spoondish dawkle dinkytoy!

Spoondish dawkle ... Well, to some extent. On the other hand, moidre boidre bellwork doidle ...

– [*'Moidre boidre ... ?' Good God, that does actually sound a bit like real conversation at last! So* . . .] Dindle dondle!

Na!

– Ha!

Na, na, na!

– [*He's making a bit of an effort, at any rate. Though what he thinks he's saying I have not the slightest idea.*] Dib dob!

Dib dob!

– [*And nor, I imagine, does he. How entirely characteristic of human communication!*] Dong dong!

Wee hee!

– Hoo ha!

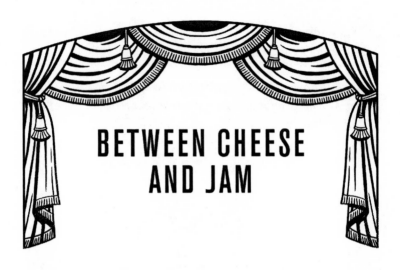

BETWEEN CHEESE
AND JAM

Hi! It's me! I've been trying and trying to phone you! I was getting worried!

– Why? What's happened?

Nothing's happened. But it kept saying engaged.

– Yes – because I was trying to phone *you*.

You were trying to phone *me*? Why? What's happened?

– Nothing's happened! I was trying to phone you, that's all.

To tell me that nothing's happened?

– No, to find out why *you* were trying to phone *me*! I was getting worried. I thought something might be the matter.

I was just worried that there might be something wrong with your phone.

– That's what you were phoning me for? Because you were worried there might be something wrong with my phone?

Yes, because if there was something wrong with your phone, and something had happened, I shouldn't have known, and I should have been worried.

– You'd have been worried? If something had happened and you hadn't known?

Of course I should have been!

– How could you have been worried if something had happened and you hadn't known?

Because I wouldn't have *known* I hadn't known!

– Exactly!

That's what I'm saying!

– Anyway, nothing *had* happened.

No. As it happens. Well, as long as you're all right . . .

– Fine.

So where are you?

– Oh no!

What? What's happened?

   – Nothing's happened! It's just that we seem to be turning into one of those couples who keep phoning each other saying 'Where are you?' 'I'm in Tesco's. Where are you?'

You're in Tesco's?

   – That's not what I'm saying. What I'm saying is . . .

You're *not* in Tesco's?

   – . . . that I don't want to start saying 'I'm in Tesco's.'

So are you in Tesco's or aren't you?

   – I *am* in Tesco's. As it happens. Why, where are you?

In Tesco's!

   – *You're* in Tesco's?

Just by the cheeses. Oh, I can see you! Over by the jam! I'm looking straight at you! I'm waving! Can you see me?

   – Of course I can see you.

I'm walking towards you . . .

   – I know, I know.

I'm almost there . . . I'm right in front of you. I'll say bye-bye, then. Speak to you soon.

THE WORDS
AND THE MUSIC

A string quartet, playing inaudibly under the noise of party conversation.

The conversation suddenly dies away, and the quartet becomes audible.

They can none of them play at all; they are just going through the motions of scraping away at their instruments.

The sound dies away. SECOND VIOLIN, VIOLA and CELLO all look at FIRST VIOLIN. He nods, and at once they all begin to play again, and to talk loudly away together to drown the sound.

FIRST VIOLIN Have you been away this year? We went to Middlesbrough – we found the most wonderful little hotel – all the waiters were drunk from morning to night – and the people up there are so charming – we were mugged twice – but with such style – you couldn't take offence – and the roof of the hotel fell in – we all ended up in this amazing hospital where the food was out of this world – the most perfectly disgusting mince for breakfast, lunch, tea and dinner – and germs, germs, the most amazing germs, everywhere . . .

SECOND VIOLIN It's funny how everything can go suddenly quiet at even the noisiest party – perhaps because someone's dropped dead in the far corner – or it may be some kind of psychic thing – because scientists do now accept that thought transmission is possible – I was reading an article about it in the *Daily Mail* – and obviously if you can catch infectious diseases over the internet as I believe you now can it must be possible to catch other things such as fish which is why there will soon be no fish fingers left in the North Sea . . .

VIOLA We paid seventeen pounds ten for our house twelve years ago and we thought it was outrageous but the Clerihews who live opposite us have just put their house on the market which is half the size of ours and with no coat cupboard to speak of – and we also have a bicycle shed that gets the sun from seven o'clock in the evening onwards, a feature the Clerihews don't have at all – and they are asking – you're not going to believe this – four million pounds, which of course they won't get but even so ours must be worth at least twenty-seven pounds fifty . . .

CELLO I'm not a great believer in faddy diets but the Bathwater Diet is quite different because you can eat and drink exactly what you like provided you also eat three dessertspoonfuls of ordinary toilet soap at the beginning

of each meal and wash it down with a gallon of dirty
bathwater and if you don't like the taste of soap you're
allowed to put toothpaste on it and if you're worried
about the bathwater then it's perfectly all right to add
disinfectant and since I went on to the diet I have no
pain in my feet at all in fact no sensation of any sort
whatsoever . . .

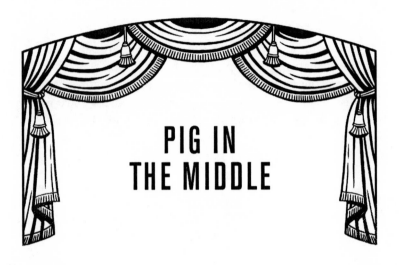

PIG IN
THE MIDDLE

(*off*) Is that you?

    – No.

(*off*) What?

    – Not me. Someone else.

(*off*) The man came about the thing while you were out.

    – The man came about the thing. What man? What
    thing?

(*off*) He says it's not the little thing round the back.

    – Not the little thing round the back. Oh.

(*off*) It's something inside.

    – Something inside. Ah.

(*off*) He says they'll have to take it away and – I don't know – but something, they'll have to do something, sort of look at it, and, I don't know, apparently it's all kind of . . . (*Enters.*) Anyway, it's not the right sort – he explained it all, I couldn't quite understand, but it'll cost about eighty pounds. I said I'd have to ask you. What do you think?

    – What do I think?

I mean, it's your thing, you'll have to decide, I don't know what to tell him . . . Did you get the things I asked you to get at the what's-it-called shop . . . ? He's going to ring tomorrow, and of course you won't be here, and I'll have to tell him *something*.

    – Right.

So what shall I tell him?

    – Who?

The man.

    – Oh, the man. Tell him the truth.

Tell him the *truth*?

    – Of course. You should always tell people the truth.

What are you talking about?

– I have not the slightest idea. I have not the slightest
idea what *I* am talking about. I have not the slightest idea what *you* are talking about. I have not the
slightest idea what either of us is talking about.

I said . . . I'm counting up to ten . . . I said, what do you
want me to do?

– What I want you to do is to start all over again. I
come through the door . . . You say, Is that you? I
say, No. You say, What? I say, Not me. Someone
else. And at that point, instead of pouring out your
heart to some complete stranger, you come into
the room to investigate. You discover that I've been
lying. It *is* me. So you place yourself opposite me,
in a good light, where I can see the movements of
your mouth, and follow the workings of your brain,
and you sit down at the table . . . You sit down at
the table. You look at me in a way that tells me that
something of importance is about to be said. You
wait till I have sat down at the table as well. You
pause a little for effect. Then you say, loudly and
clearly . . .

The man came about the thing.

– The man came about the thing. Good. *Good.* Now
we're getting somewhere. I look interested. I raise
my eyebrows. I nod. And I say, 'What man came
about what thing?'

What man? What thing? What do you mean? You know what man! You know what thing!

– Curiously, no.

Yes you do. The thing on the . . .

– Oh, *no*! You mean the thing on the . . . ?

Yes! The thing on the . . .

– And he said *what*?

He said it's not the little thing round the back . . .

– Of course it's the little thing round the back!

He said it's something inside.

– Something inside? *What* something inside?

I don't know!

– You didn't ask him? He said, 'It's something inside,' and you didn't ask him *what* something inside?

You ask him!

– How *can* I ask him! He's not here!

No! He's never here when you're here! *You're* never here when *he's* here!

– He's never here when I'm here and I'm never here
   when he's here for a very simple reason . . .

I'm always left to run messages back and forth between
the two of you!

 – Because he waits in the street out there until he sees
   me go out of the door.

It's got nothing to do with me! I don't know anything
about it!

 – He waits for me to be out of the house because he
   knows that I understand what he says.

It's your thing!

 – He knows that when he tells me that it's something
   inside I will ask him *what* thing inside . . .

I *did* ask him what thing inside!

 – . . . And he will tell me . . .

He *told* me!

 – . . . And I will be listening . . .

I *was* listening!

 – . . . And it will be nonsense, because it's not the
   thing inside, it's never the thing inside, it's always,
   always, always the little thing round the back . . .

I *told* him that!

> – . . . And when he says it will cost – how much? – to
> fix . . .

I've no idea!

> – . . . eighty pounds to fix, plus VAT, then he knows . . .

He knows you'll fly into one of your rages.

> – . . . And he knows that if he tells *you* that it's the
> thing inside you will not have the faintest idea what
> he is talking about, and you will believe it . . .

I'm just telling you what he said!

> – . . . And you will repeat it to me . . .

And you'll fly into one of your rages – but not with him
– with me!

> – . . . And we will have *another* row about it . . .

It's always the same!

> – . . . And maybe, he thinks, maybe, maybe, this time
> it will be a row of such epic, such terminal violence
> that I will walk out of the house and so not be here
> to ring him up and tell him that in my humble
> opinion it is *not* the thing inside . . .

You *never* ring him up! *He* rings *me* up!

– . . . And you will let him do the thing inside . . .

Last time it was the thing underneath . . .

– . . . And it will cost eighty pounds, plus VAT, which he knows will net him a profit of approximately seventy-nine pounds and ninety-three pence, plus for all I know the VAT as well . . .

If *you* want to argue with him, *you* argue with him!

– . . . And maybe, he thinks, I will not even be here when he brings it back . . .

You're *never* here when he brings it back!

– . . . And it still doesn't work . . .

I'll be the one who has to tell him!

– . . . So perhaps this time I will not make him take it away again . . .

You're never the one who has to make him take it away again!

– . . . And perhaps, he thinks, as he hides out there, waiting for me to leave the house, perhaps this time, for once, he will not have to do what he has had to do on all nine hundred and ninety-nine previous occasions . . .

I'm the one who has to tell him *everything*!

    – . . . Which is what I told you to tell him to do in the
      first place: the little thing – round – the back.

What's this you've bought?

    – That? What you told me to buy.

I told you *not* to buy that sort!

    – They hadn't got the other sort.

Of course they've got the other sort!

    – They said they *haven't* got the other sort.

You always say they say that!

    – Because that's what they always say!

Because you always go to the place inside! You never go
to the little place round the back . . . !

LET ME TELL YOU A LITTLE ABOUT MYSELF

Hello? Is that the Council . . . ? Oh good – though I'm afraid I have to confess that I voted for the other lot. Well, I did at the local elections – not because I'm in favour of their policies – in fact I voted for your lot at the General Election, or rather I would have done, if I'd been able to get to the polling station that day, but unfortunately my sister was taken ill, and I had to . . .

Sorry? Which department do I want . . . ? No, of course, I realise how busy you are . . . I agree – I only wish *I'd* got time to sit here chatting, too. That's the awful thing about life today. No one ever has a chance to sit down and . . .

Yes, of course. So sorry. Well, I want to talk to the department that deals with old sofas. Collecting them and disposing of them – though what they do with them, whether they recycle them or whether they pass them on to families in need, because I know there are a lot of people in the world who would be glad of . . .

I beg your pardon . . . ? Oh, is this someone else I'm talking to now? Is this the department that deals with old sofas . . . ? Oh, good, wonderful. I should be *so* grateful if you could help me. I realise what an awful job it must be, dragging heavy sofas about – though on the other hand you must often get interesting glimpses into the lives of the people who are getting rid of the sofas – which is something that I think I should find really rather . . .

A sofa, yes – I have a sofa I want to get rid of. I'm sorry to have to ask you, but it's become very worn, and I kept putting off doing anything about it, putting it off and putting it off, and then last Tuesday, I think it was – no, Wednesday, because it was the day Mrs Plorey comes – I saw a new sofa that I quite liked the look of, in that new shop in the High Street – well, I say new, but it's been there for several years now – though I didn't like the manner of the girl who was selling it . . . So impatient, a lot of shop assistants these days. You try to have a friendly conversation with them, and they really don't . . .

The sofa . . . ? Yes, of course. I know I tend to wander off the point if I'm not checked. People have been telling me about it ever since I was a little girl – I remember the history teacher saying she thought I ought to give the subject up, because I was never going to get further than the first year I happened to . . .

The sofa, the sofa! Yes! Well, it's got a flowered pattern – wild roses mixed with honeysuckle – but rather impressionistic – and it was originally marked at seven hundred and ninety-nine pounds – which I thought was *far* too much – only then I saw it was in the sale, and . . .

No, no – the *new* sofa. The *new* sofa was in the sale . . . The old sofa . . . ?

I'm so sorry! Obviously it's the old sofa you're more interested in, since that's the one you're so kindly going to dispose of! Well, it is, as I say, rather *worn* – particularly where the cat has scratched it. I've tried to provide Timmy with other things to sharpen his claws on – but you know what cats are like – they're so difficult to have a reasonable conversation with – they just yawn at you! And then of course my children used to jump on it – they're grown-up now – one of them's a barrister, but then of course she always had the gift of the gab – and the younger one makes little painted eggcups and napkin rings with most unusual designs . . .

The what . . . ? The details? Well, some of them are based on graffiti she's found – not rude ones, of course, she wouldn't use rude ones . . .

Of the *sofa* . . . ? The details of the *sofa* . . . ? Of course. I'm wandering off the point again! Just the way the history teacher said! And of course it wasn't just the history teacher! The maths teacher said that once I'd started on a sum . . .

The sofa. Well, it was originally left me by my aunt . . .

On my father's side . . . ? No, no, my mother's . . . !

Oh – it wasn't a serious question? No, no – but you're right! This was my Aunt Jessica, not my Aunt Pat! The only thing my Aunt Pat left me was a small china clock – which was worth virtually nothing – and which had stopped years before, in any case – because she'd had a great falling out with my mother . . .

When? Oh, in I think 1937 – when was the Coronation . . . ?

No, not of the present Queen! Of Edward VIII. Or do I mean George VI? I've got a commemorative mug somewhere . . .

On the mantelpiece? No, I think it's at the top of the bedroom cupboard somewhere . . . No, no, not the front bedroom – the back bedroom . . .

You *don't* want to know which bedroom . . . ? I'm sorry, I thought you asked me if it was the front bedroom, and I said . . . You were joking? Oh, how sweet of you. Because I just thought, you probably like to know a bit about the people you're dealing with . . .

Are you still there . . . ? Are you all right? You sound a bit strange. Too much to do, I expect, like all the rest of us! Are you married? Or should I say, Are you in a relationship? Do you have children, on top of everything else . . . ?

The sofa, yes. Stick to the sofa . . . No, of course, not – it's not at all impertinent of you to ask about the size. That's something you obviously need to know, and I only wish I could tell you the answer in so many feet and inches. Or metres, of course! It's quite *long*, I can tell you that. It won't go into the space between the fireplace and the door – not unless I move the bookcase, and if I put the bookcase in the hall then what should I do with the hatstand . . . ?

No, no, I understand . . . Large, yes – put down 'large' . . . And the address . . . ? Certainly. You must have the address, obviously, and as it happens it's a very easy one to remember, because the number of the house is exactly twice the age of the present Queen – or it was when she was seventy, only . . . Yes – 140. Exactly. 140 Sunnydeep Lane, which was a very nice street, until they built those flats at the corner . . .

When will I be in . . . ? Well, any day this week, except Thursday morning, when I'm going to be out visiting an old friend of mine who's had a most unusual accident. She fell off her chair, apparently in a deep sleep, while I was actually on the phone talking to her . . .

AUGHT FOR NAUGHT

A banqueting hall. The KING OF GREENLAND, *various* PRINCES *and divers* LORDS. *Also* GENTLEMEN IN DINNER JACKETS, *and their* LADIES.

GREENLAND
A welcome first to all our noble guests
Who banquet with our royal self tonight!
Though we be sworn foes since time began,
Ay, have contended much on bloody fields
For cursed crowns, and never tarried yet
To stoop to treachery of every kind –
The posset slyly drugged, the poisoned rapier,
The lover's hug that hides the gruesome blade –
Now say we this to all assembled here:
Enough of battle! Down, the dogs of war!
Tonight for one short hour let us be friends,
And we shall drink until our heads go round,
And not a man be fit to draw his sword!
Which being so, I shall disclose at last

The small surprise I have in store for you
That waits beneath the silver covers here.
So welcome, royal brother from Navarre!

NAVARRE
Much thanks, most royal Greenland, I return!

GREENLAND
Hail, Prince of Muscovy, and Tartary.
Hail, Fife! And sweet Dunoon! Clackmannan, hail!

MUSCOVY
The Prince of Muscovy hurls hails back!

TARTARY
From Tartary come hails more num'rous yet!

FIFE
From Fife!

DUNOON
              And from Dunoon!

CLACKMANNAN
                          Clackmannan, too!

GREENLAND
And a specially warm welcome I extend
To good my lord the Baron Tethering,
The Chairman of Consolidated Ales,
Whose generous sponsorship of th' performing arts,
Made possible the production here tonight.

TETHERING

I thank Your Majesty, great Greenland's king,
And welcome in my turn the many guests,
Invited by Consolidated Ales
To join us at our banquet here tonight.
We trust they will enjoy the food and wine.
But more, we hope they will appreciate
The chance to make a little history.
For this is more than just another feast.
It is a venture, surely quite unique,
That marks a bold new milestone on the road
To bring the worlds of art and business closer.
You may have wondered why so many here,
In these most ancient, far-off, gloomy times,
Have donned black tie and faint embarrassed smiles.
Be not perplexed. All things shall be revealed.
For many years Consolidated Ales
Have done their humble best to lend support
To foster excellence in th' performing arts.
Have offered generous grants and sponsorship,
Have watered half the world with chilled champagne,
Hired rooms for lavish corporate entertainment,
Made free with mention of our well-known name.
Yet still we seek new ways to help the arts,
New ways to entertain our jaded guests.
Producers tell us that they find it hard
To pay a cast of more than half a dozen;
How can they stage a mighty banquet scene
With half a dozen players? Unless, unless –
We hurl our guests into the thick of things,
The very furnace where the gold is cast,
And entertain them on the stage itself!
Two birds fall conjoint victim to one stone!

The stage fills up; the guests are tickled pink;
And once again I claim a corporate first
By greeting your good selves in noble verse.

GREENLAND
Most humble thanks.

GUESTS
                    Hear hear! Hear hear!

GREENLAND
                                    And on
We hasten to despatch the pressing business
Of this our pregnant scene. (*Draws.*) En garde, Navarre!

NAVARRE
What's this?

CLACKMANNAN
            'Tis naked treachery!

NAVARRE
                                Ho, guards!
Guards, ho! Help, help! Mon dieu! I am undone!

CLACKMANNAN
Nay, Scotland draws and stands beside Navarre!

FIFE
And where Clackmannan leads, shall Fife fall short?
I draw! Draw thou, Dunoon!

DUNOON

Dunoon is up!

MUSCOVY

Shall peaceful Muscovy sit idly by
When noble cousin Greenland stands alone,
And murd'rous thanes from unknown Scottish boroughs
Already leap with swordsman's saucy foot
Upon the purlieus of the festive board?

TARTARY

No, never, nor shall Tartary neither!

NAVARRE

Ho!

CLACKMANNAN

Ha!

FIFE

Ho!

SIR SPOKESWOOD

But first, if I may break in here,
This might perhaps be an appropriate moment,
Before the clash of swords becomes too loud –
And as I understand much blood will flow
Before we reach the coffee and cigars,
With many eyes put out and ears cut off,
And served with boiled heads, in brandy sauce! –
Perhaps, before all this, I might just say
A word of thanks, on all the guests' behalf,
To my old friend and yours, Lord Tethering,

For everything Consolidated Ales
Have done to make this frankly gruesome play
An agreeable occasion for us all.

GUESTS
Hear hear!

GREENLAND
                    Now back to all the evil plots
Of naughty Fife, the wicked stratagems
Of heartless black Dunoon.

CLACKMANNAN
                                    Have at you now!

DUNOON
So die, Navarre!

NAVARRE
                        Die thou, Dunoon!

MUSCOVY
                                            But soft!
Observe the Queen!

TARTARY
                            What ails the Queen?

GREENLAND
                                            The Queen!

They stand.

OMNES
The Queen!

They drink.

QUEEN
My lords, much thanks. 'Tis truly naught.
A little poison in the wine, no more.
Some slight confusion overcame my mind;
I had forgot which was the fatal draught,
The claret, or th' New Zealand Sauvignon.

GREENLAND
Attend the Queen. Explain which bottle's which.
Yet stay! What see I now! What horror's here?
Who can he be, this ghastly bloody man
That rises most untimely from his seat
And bends his lips in counterfeited mirth,
And threats to give dread utterance to his thoughts?

SIR SPOKESWOOD
'Tis merely I again, Sir Spokeswood Geech.
One most important thing I did forget –
And should amend before we are involved
In what's to happen next, which I believe
Involves the entrance of some sort of ghost!

GREENLAND
Ay, there it stands, the ghost of John o'Gaunt!

NAVARRE
Most foully murdered by this upstart king . . .

SIR SPOKESWOOD
Yes, yes, but first things first! I have to thank
Our gracious hostess, Lady Tethering.
'Twas Lady Tethering who chose the cat'rers
And she who did the charming flower arrangements.
My lady Tethering – can words express
Our gratitude for all your time and skill?

GREENLAND
No, they could not.

NAVARRE
                              No, no!

MUSCOVY
                                            No, nor they could.

TARTARY
Were you to speak a thousand years or more.

GREENLAND
So, there it stands, the ghost of John o'Gaunt . . .

SIR SPOKESWOOD
I do apologise. Please – carry on.

GREENLAND
Well, there it stands, the ghost of John o'Gaunt . . .

SIR SPOKESWOOD
'Twas best, I felt, to interrupt you then,
Before we all got slightly too involved.

GREENLAND
Yes, there it stands, the ghost of John o'Gaunt . . .

MR M. K. HOPPER, SOUTHERN AREA MANAGER, MAGIFROTH
BREWING EQUIPMENT
If I might trouble you – the bottle there . . .

GREENLAND
The bottle, certainly . . . And now, the ghost,
The fearful spectre that affrights our feast . . .

MR ELSWORTHY, OF ELSWORTHY & ELSWORTHY
And seeing ghosts reminds me of the time
When someone in Consolidated Ales
Who shall be nameless, though some of you will guess
Exactly who I mean . . . Or am I wrong?
And was it someone else? Well, never mind.
Now this will make you laugh . . . On second thoughts,
'Nuff said. I'll spare the wretched victim's blushes!
Suffice to say he is not unacquainted
With, yes, ahem, a certain lady here!

GREENLAND
Meanwhile the fearful ghost before me waits . . .

MRS BOOTLE, THE WIFE OF MR BOOTLE, OF BOTTLE,
BOOTLE, & BEETLE
And have you been away somewhere this year?
Or maybe I have asked you that before?

MRS ELSWORTHY
We went to Thailand.

[169]

MRS BOOTLE

                    Thailand, yes, you said.

MRS ELSWORTHY

We found this marvellous place that no one knows.

MRS BOOTLE

This marvellous little place – yes, yes, you said.

GREENLAND

How thrilling. Now, to change the subject slightly . . .

MR HOPPER

Great Scott, what's this delightful-looking dish?

LADY GEECH

I'm told it's someone's grandmother, chopped fine,
And served with lightly marinated toads
And boiled eye of newt, in garlic sauce.

MRS BOOTLE

Oh, such a treat! So hard these days to get
A free-range grandmother with any taste.

SIR SPOKESWOOD

Oh, yes, they always do you awfully well,
Consolidated Ales.

MR HOPPER

                    Oh, awfully well!
I'm just so tired of all those endless nights
Of dreary salmon mousse and *Traviata*
That International Beers keep serving up.

GREENLAND
I'll go aside, and run upon my sword.

TETHERING
And that reminds me: to assist the staff
And make it easier to serve the meal,
We would ask all those due to end up dead
To help us, if they would, and go ahead
As quickly and as quietly as they may
To meet their tragic end without delay.
I thank you.

GREENLAND ETC.
       Thank you.

They die in various ways.

TETHERING
              My most humble thanks.
Take up the bodies, and, our duty done,
Roll back the carpet and let's have some fun!

POST-MORTEM

Oh, God, you weren't in tonight, were you? Why do people always come on the wrong night?

No, kind of you to make the effort. Much appreciated. And sweet of you to come round afterwards! Would you like a drink? We're all having a drink to try to cheer ourselves up. We were so rubbish tonight! And something went horribly wrong in that bit in the second half. Did you notice? The bit where everyone's yakking away, and it's supposed to be all sort of whatever . . . I don't know . . . Did you understand it . . . ? No, nor do we.

Actually none of us have a clue what we're doing from one moment to the next, so the whole thing's a total nightmare, we're all exhausted.

Also, you were a really rubbish audience tonight! Where did they dig you lot up? In some mediaeval plague-pit?

You should have been here last Thursday! No, last Wednesday. The matinee. Tiny house – only one of them! – but they really loved it!

Why don't you come back and read it again last Wednesday?

Author's Note

Two of these sketches, 'A Pleasure Shared' and 'Outside Story', have appeared in earlier collections, but have never been staged. Another two, 'Finishing Touches' and 'Pig in the Middle', have been staged, in a touring production of *Alarms and Excursions*, but have never been published.

About the Author

Michael Frayn was born in London in 1933 and began his career as a journalist on the *Guardian* and the *Observer*. One of the few English writers to achieve success as both novelist and playwright, his three most recent novels, *Headlong*, *Spies*, and *Skios*, were all nominated for the Booker Prize, while *Noises Off* (first produced in New York in 1983, revived in 2001, and due to be revived again in 2015) was recently voted Britain's second favourite play, and *Copenhagen* won the Tony Award for Best Play. His first five novels, all long recognized as classics in Great Britain, are also published by Valancourt Books.